How to
Go Viral
and **Reach**
Millions

Top Persuasion Secrets from
Social Media Superstars,
Jesus, Shakespeare, Oprah,
and Even Donald Trump

JOSEPH ROMM

LUMINARE PRESS
WWW.LUMINAREPRESS.COM

How to Go Viral and Reach Millions
© 2018 Joseph Romm

Printed in the United States of America

Cover Design: Claire Flint Last

Luminare Press
438 Charnelton St., Suite 101
Eugene, OR 97401
www.luminarepress.com

LCCN: 2018944160
ISBN: 978-1-944733-77-3

To Antonia
For giving me the gift of
seeing the world anew through your eyes, and
for teaching me more than I could possibly teach you

TABLE OF CONTENTS

INTRODUCTION
The Five Rules of Going Viral 1

CHAPTER ONE
How to Be a Winner like Trump without
Being a Loser like Trump 17

CHAPTER TWO
How to Tell a Viral Story:
Word of Mouth from Jesus to Lincoln to Oprah 29

CHAPTER THREE
Short Words Win, Short Words Sell 49

CHAPTER FOUR
Repeat, Repeat, Repeat:
Only Memorable Memes Go Viral 59

CHAPTER FIVE
Irony: The Viral Twist We Can't Resist from
Socrates to Seinfeld 75

CHAPTER SIX
"Do Not Throw Away Your Shot":
Foreshadowing, *Hamilton*, and Virality 95

CHAPTER SEVEN
Metaphors Are like Warp Drive:
The Viral Power of Proto-Stories 111

CHAPTER EIGHT

It's the Headline, Stupid: Why Big Data and
Message Testing Mean Life or Death in the
Facebook Era 131

CHAPTER NINE

James Cameron, 60 Minutes, Years of Living
Dangerously: Revealing the Secrets Behind the
Most Viral Videos 149

CHAPTER TEN

Amazon, Branding, and Personal Character:
How to Have a Viral Impact in Your
Professional Life 163

CHAPTER ELEVEN

Resisting Trumpism and Russian Cyberwarfare:
Don't Bring a Knife to a Gun Fight 183

Epilogue and Epitaph: My Brother's Keeper 203

Shout Outs 212

References 215

Index 221

The Five Rules of Going Viral

When you plant a fertile meme in my mind you literally parasitize my brain, turning it into a vehicle for the meme's propagation in just the way that a virus may parasitize the genetic mechanism of a host cell.

—Richard Dawkins, *The Selfish Gene*, 1976

Virality isn't born. It's made.

—Jonah Berger, *Contagious: Why Things Catch On*, 2013

At every step, the Russians used Facebook's own tools to make sure their propaganda was as effective as possible ... to get real-time results on which types of ad campaigns were reaching their target audience or which posts were getting the most engagement with viewers.

—*The New York Times*, February 17, 2018

Back in 2010, when my daughter was three, she started saying, "blah, blah, blah." I was okay with her repeating things she heard—if she used them correctly. So I asked her if she knew what "blah, blah, blah" meant. She paused and said, "It's when Daddy says something that doesn't matter." Dang. She did know what it meant.

Until I had a daughter, I never realized just how often I said things that don't matter. But since then, I have focused all my efforts on figuring out which of my communications matter and which don't.

And by *matter*, I mean mattering to my audience (or your audience) whether we're talking to a daughter, a date, a boss, a coworker, a client, our Twitter and Facebook followers, the media, a crowd at a conference, or friends and family at a funeral. This book will teach you *virality*: the science and art of creating content that does not disappear after you speak or write it, but instead is memorable enough to live on. The ultimate goal is to create messages that have a direct and engaging emotional impact on listeners or readers, so they have the potential to spread fast and far, to go "viral."

You'll learn the newest, most important secrets of consistently generating viral online content—words, images, or videos that are seen and shared by hundreds of thousands and eventually even millions of people, which is something my colleagues and I routinely achieve in three different organizations. My top post of 2017 had a half million direct views, which means more than ten million people probably saw the headline or some part of the story. Not bad for an article on climate change. Imagine the reach and impact you could have when you learn these secrets.

You will also learn the secrets of going viral in your professional life: how to communicate your ideas in the most memorable and persuasive way, consistent with your personal story, to build and grow your "brand," to maximize your impact—so you can stand out from the crowd no matter your passion or profession.

We'll learn these secrets from the best practitioners and social media mavens I know, as well as some of the world's greatest masters of creating viral content—Jesus, Shakespeare, Lincoln, Martin Luther King, song-writers like Lady Gaga and *Hamilton*'s Lin-Manuel Miranda, Barack Obama,

Oprah, and even Donald Trump. I say "even Donald Trump" because many people I talk to—especially Democrats, environmentalists, and scientists—remain puzzled by Trump's 2016 victory, draw the wrong conclusions, or worst of all, mistakenly believe there is nothing to be learned from a man as flawed as Trump.

But as we will see, Trump and his digital campaign team (along with the Russians and fake-news sites like Breitbart) mastered virality, whereas Hillary Clinton explicitly rejected it. That explains much of why he is now President and she isn't. *Indeed, until and unless progressives fully understand and embrace viral messaging, our democracy and the future of a livable climate are at risk.*

Like a lot of people, I spent most of my life guessing which of my communications mattered, which were truly memorable and effective. But the good news is that the revolutions in social media, information technology, and brain science now make it possible to stop *guessing* and start *knowing* which communications matter. We now know the best strategies and tactics—and they were not taught to you in high school or college.

If you and the organizations you work with use the secrets in my book as the cornerstone of your messaging and media strategy, then you'll maximize your chances of going viral. And you won't be trying to shout into the roar of Niagara Falls like everyone else.

THE FIVE RULES OF GOING VIRAL: HOW TO BE CLICKY *AND* STICKY

The good news is also the bad news: Those who do understand the secrets of viral messaging are flooding the system, inundating it with both good news and bad news that grabs your initial attention (clicky) and then keeps it (sticky).

You can cut through the clutter by embracing these five rules for consistently creating content that can go viral:

---

1. STORY: Tell a compelling story—but use the simple And-But-Therefore formula.
2. FIGURES OF SPEECH: Use the most unforgettable figures of speech, especially repetition, irony, and metaphor.
3. EMOTION: Trigger one of three activating emotions that trigger content sharing.
4. MEMORABLE ELEMENTS: Select the most memorable words, phrases, and stories.
5. TESTING: Embrace message testing and tested messages

This book explains in detail how to wield these five weapons to become an influence ninja.

If you're not doing all five—and very, very few people or organizations are—then your message is at high risk of being drowned out by those who are. If you're not doing all five, then you are at high risk of being ignored or forgotten amidst the deafening drumbeat of our 24-7 news and social media cycle, a drumbeat that Trump has amplified and sped up to an intensity previously unimaginable.

These five strategies are proven to work by leading experts at making viral content, including my colleagues and me. These five strategies are also proven to work by three separate sciences: the latest marketing research, social science, and brain studies.

A central point of this book—perhaps the single most important thing to understand and internalize, to get in your gut—is that these five strategies are in fact all basically just one over-arching strategy. This is the Grand Unified Theory (GUT) of going viral: **If you want to be as memorable as possible, you need a message that triggers the right emotions, and that is most consistently achieved by telling a simple, compelling story using the figures of speech. Those are the most tested winning messages over the many thousands of years of human civilization, and, the science increasingly tells us, the many tens of thousands of years it took homo sapiens to evolve our mastery of language. When you test multiple messages online—when you crowd-source your headlines, your over-arching message, and other content—you can learn the specific words and images that your audience finds most clicky and sticky.**

From the dawn of language eons ago to now, the most viral messages have always been stories told with the figures of speech that trigger key emotions and stick in the memory such as metaphor, irony, and repetition, but also others such as hyperbole and apophasis (pretended denial), two of Donald Trump's favorites. The figures were the focus of my 2012 book, *Language Intelligence*.

These viral messages include humanity's best known and most retold stories which have literally spread by word-of-mouth and stood the test of time, such as the heroic journeys of the great epic poems like Homer's *Iliad* and *Odyssey*. The stories of the Bible embodied the strategies above—and they are arguably the most successful and influential collection of viral content ever created.

Today, the most viral messages are also stories told with the figures of speech that trigger key emotions and stick in the memory. We call them pop songs and hip-hop. They comprise 95 of the top 100 *YouTube* videos of all time. There's much to learn from viral songwriters—our modern-day bards. For instance, Lin-Manuel Miranda's game-changing hip-hop musical, *Hamilton*, is the quintessence of the five rules of virality. I think anyone who is serious about mastering these skills should memorize the whole musical.

The Greeks figured out some twenty-five centuries ago that the figures of speech were the memory tricks the ancient bards used to remember their long epic poems and songs—tricks that also made sure the audience remembered them. The Greeks further understood that persuasive and memorable storytelling using the figures was the best way to be emotionally compelling. Here is Aristotle in his classic text on the art of persuasion, *Rhetoric*, discussing the importance of mimicking natural speech:

> Your language will be appropriate if it expresses emotion and character.... To express emotion, you'll employ the language of anger in speaking of outrage; the language of disgust and discreet reluctance to utter a word when speaking of impiety or foulness; the language of exultation for a tale of glory.

What makes people believe us and trust us? As Aristotle goes on to say, "This aptness of language is one thing that makes people believe in the truth of your story." He links specific figures of speech with specific emotional states. For instance, he noted that *hyperbole*—extravagant exaggeration—is used by angry men, so it's no surprise Trump's use of hyperbole was central to his emotional connection with so many angry voters. Clinton's rejection of figurative speech is one reason she had difficulty making an emotional connection with so many voters.

Modern brain science confirms this ancient wisdom. As Kendall Haven sums up the key findings in his book,

Story Proof: The Science Behind the Startling Power of Stories: "Emotional information triggers memory." Of course, you don't need studies to know emotions cause vivid memory. You just have to pause and recall your most memorable moments to realize that what is welded onto your memory are the moments attached to the strongest emotions: your first kiss, a shameful or embarrassing action, your pride and joy in a big victory or achievement by you or your child, a moment of sheer terror, the time you felt betrayed, the death of a close relative, and on and on. Emotions tell us which events are worth remembering.

THE ANIMAL THAT NEEDS STORIES

Another key conclusion from recent brain research is that evolution has wired our brains to think in narrative. Stories are how we make sense of the world, how we understand our role in it, and how we create meaning in our lives. Indeed, the word *narrative* comes from the Latin *narrare:* to tell, relate, recount, which in turn comes from Proto-Indo-European root *gnō-*, meaning "to know," which is the root of words such as cognition, ignorant, and know. Our brains have evolved to know, to think, and to explain through stories.

Since our brains are wired for stories, it's only natural that the figures of speech—the core elements of any emotionally compelling and memorable story—turn out to, "constitute basic schemes by which people conceptualize their experience and the external world," as cognitive scientist Raymond Gibbs, Jr. put it in his 1994 book, *The Poetics of Mind.* We think in figures, so the figures can be used to change our thinking.

Thus, being memorable—through emotionally resonant storytelling—is not just crucial to going viral. It's also crucial to being persuasive. "One of the brain's subconscious rules of thumb is that easily recalled things are true," as one

Washington Post article discussing the extensive social science research on this "truth effect" put it. This truth explains the key role repetition plays in both persuasion and virality.

Since deliberative thinking requires so much metabolic energy—and takes so much time—humans have developed a great many mental shortcuts to make sense of things, to figure out the best strategy when actions and decisions need to be made quickly. Generally, those shortcuts are a form of pattern matching. Does my current problem or situation resemble one I have seen or heard about before?

As we evolved, the brain "was forced to rely on tricks to enlarge memory and speed computation," explained the acclaimed biologist Edward O. Wilson in his book *Biophilia*. Hence, the human mind "specializes on analogy and metaphor, on a sweeping together of chaotic sensory experience into workable categories labeled by words and stacked into hierarchies for quick recovery."

The best stories are the highest form of pattern matching and analogy precisely because they are the most detailed descriptions of people's behavior and decisions—and their consequences. That explains their power. Indeed, beginning in early childhood, we'll watch, listen to, and read our favorite stories time and time again, and we'll eagerly embrace new stories, especially ones with our favorite characters. It's been said that humans are "the storytelling animal," but we're really "the story-needing animal." We need to tell them, yes, but we also need to hear them—again and again.

The problem is your brain can be hacked by taking advantage of these very shortcuts to lead you astray, to lead you to make a bad decision. This is seduction, the dark side of persuasive and memorable speech, the dark side of virality. One of the goals of this book is to expose the devious devices used by dangerous demagogues, crafty Casanovas, and sneaky salesmen. The language intelligence needed to thwart those ultra-subtle seducers comes naturally to very few. To be resisted and debunked, their verbal tricks must be made explicit. If you don't debunk a demagogue like Trump or a climate science denier correctly—and most people, including most journalists, don't—then you will only help their message go viral.

Few people are taught any of this in high school and college. Worse, most of us have been taught to be as unmemorable and unpersuasive as possible. It has taken me a quarter-century to unlearn almost everything I was taught about communications on my journey to get a Ph.D. in physics, particularly the notion that educated people should be as unemotional and literal-minded as possible when writing and speaking.

That so many people are terrified of public speaking is more evidence of the failure of our modern educational system. We evolved an amazing ability and need to tell and to hear memorable, emotionally compelling stories. If you follow the five rules of going viral—and throw in one simple, but ingenious hack from storytelling guru Randy Olson—you'll be emulating history's most famous public speakers. You will quickly surpass the vast majority of people in speaking skill, and any fears you have about telling stories in public or delivering a eulogy will start to fade.

Significantly, the world of communications completely changed in the last few years, during the very time I was trying to make my content go viral. Because of this revolution, my colleagues and I now have access to powerful but inexpensive tools to help maximize the chances our content is both clicky and sticky.

If you use the same tools and rules that we use, your content will be clickier and stickier, too.

THE STORIES BEHIND THIS BOOK

This is the first book to reveal all of these secrets. The only reason I've been able to write it is that I've been incredibly fortunate to work with and learn from cutting-edge experts from three organizations at the forefront of that revolution: ThinkProgress, the leading progressive news and opinion website, The Years Project, the multimedia home of viral climate and energy videos, and New Frontier Data, the leading "big data" firm providing actionable analysis in cannabis. The views expressed in this book belong solely to me, however, and not necessarily to these organizations.

They each have very different stories and very different approaches to creating viral content. But, as we'll see, you can go viral online in many ways, just as you can go viral in life in many ways.

My online viral story began in 2006, when I founded ClimateProgress.org, a project of the Center for American Progress Action Fund. Within a few years, it had gone viral. *Time* magazine named it one of the "Best Blogs of 2010," and one of "The top five blogs *Time* writers read daily." *Nature* called it "perhaps the world's most influential political climate-change blog." *The New York Times* columnist Tom Friedman called it the "indispensible blog."

A few years ago, ClimateProgress became the climate section of the Center's broader news website, ThinkProgress, which was founded in 2005. So much of my success over the years was built upon the advice and expertise of the ThinkProgress team. Since that merger, I've been able to work directly with the world-class writers, editors, and social media mavens under the leadership of Editor-in-Chief, Judd Legum—a team that created one of "the ten most popular news" sites online, as ranked by *Lifewire* in 2017.

Previously, my best posts had tens of thousands of page views. But by 2017, the very best had hundreds of thousands. The all-important headlines were being seen by millions of people through social media platforms like Twitter and Facebook, as well as Reddit, Yahoo, and Google. In March 2013, ClimateProgress had a combined following on Facebook and Twitter of 50,000, which dwarfed the number of followers on the sites that deny climate science. But just five years later, ClimateProgress has 280,000 followers on Facebook and another 200,000 on Twitter. ThinkProgress has an even more remarkable 1.8 million followers on Facebook and 850,000 on Twitter.

By 2017, headline testing, the equivalent of having our readers crowdsource the best headline in real time, had become a core strategy for generating the most viral content. Testing allows sites to identify the headline people are most likely to click on and the one that keeps the most people sticking around to actually read the post.

On a busy day, we might test a hundred headlines with our readers. But Donald Trump's presidential campaign was ultimately testing 50,000 to 60,000 ads a day on Facebook, as explained by Brad Parscale, the campaign's digital director (who is now manager of Trump's 2020 reelection campaign). Now *that's* message testing. It allowed them to raise a quarter-billion dollars on Facebook, while at the same time honing and perfecting their message for every conceivable voter group. Post-election analysis found that the handful of swing states where Trump exceeded his public polling numbers, the states that made him President, were precisely those states where his social media engagement was the highest. Moreover, thanks to the FBI and our intelligence agencies, we are learning the crucial and symbiotic role the Russians played in turning Trump's viral messages into an epidemic.

My second story begins in April 2010, when I met one of the few billion-dollar storytellers of our time, director James Cameron, backstage at a huge Earth Day rally on the Mall in Washington, DC. Knowing that he was going to be there and hoping we would connect over our shared concerns about climate change, I brought my new book of blog posts, *Straight Up*, and asked Earth Day founder Denis Hayes to introduce us.

In person, Cameron is every bit as charismatic and brilliant as I'd imagined the director of so many of my favorite movies would be. I was only able to talk with him briefly and barely slipped my book into his hands before he was swamped with admirers and his attention sailed off. I felt even more dejected when a half hour later I happened to notice he had left my book on a nearby table where he had been holding court.

I went looking for him among the backstage crowd and finally found him chatting in the speaker's ready room. I waited for a lull in the conversation, took out my book and said with the biggest possible smile, "Who do I have to give this to so it doesn't get left on a table when you're swarmed by fans?" Cameron chuckled and pointed to the lovely woman sitting next to him, his wife Suzy Amis. We all talked for longer this time, and he promised to read the book.

Months passed, then in August I got a call from a member of his team inviting me to spend some time with him in Aspen, Colorado. As we'll see, that second meeting ultimately led to my being part of the team behind the Emmy-winning TV docuseries, *Years of Living Dangerously*, which *The Guardian* called "perhaps the most important climate change multimedia communication endeavor in history."

By 2017, The Years Project team led by Joel Bach and David Gelber—two former *60 Minutes* producers with a combined 13 Emmys—was creating online viral videos that were routinely getting tens of millions of views a month on Facebook. And they were all on climate change, which is hardly the sexiest or most inherently viral subject.

My third story began in the spring of 2014, when an online dating site I was using ran its massive amount of data on singles in the Washington, DC area through its various algorithms—and said I was a 99% match with a brilliant Cuban-Italian entrepreneur named Giadha De Carcer. But that match, made possible by "big data," did not lead to romance. Instead, it led to my becoming an advisor to her start-up company in 2015, New Frontier Data, which under her leadership has, in just three years, become the leading "big data" firm providing accurate analysis in the cannabis sector.

Its brand has gone viral, as it has become the go-to source for the industry, investors, regulators, academics, and the media seeking the highest quality information in this rapidly expanding industry. For example, New Frontier was quoted in over 16,000 news articles in 2017 alone, an effective media reach of five billion people, and the equivalent of $46 million in "earned" (or free) media.

For me, it's been an eye-opening lesson in an essential element of modern virality—"big data." Big data is an ill-defined term that OxfordDictionaries.com calls "extremely large data sets that may be analyzed computationally to reveal patterns, trends, and associations, especially relating to human behavior and interactions." The key phrase is "reveal patterns."

Pattern matching, as noted earlier, is one of humanity's defining features. Our brains have evolved to make sense of the staggering amount of data and information we receive through our senses every second, every minute, every hour, every day. Our brains have a unique ability to rapidly figure out which information is relevant and then to process that information in real time at a very high level, including through metaphors and stories. That ability is crucial to understanding the world around us and our role in it, crucial to helping us make everyday decisions as well as predictions about the consequences of our actions and what the future may hold.

But it's not unique any more. Computers can beat the best chess players and the best *Jeopardy!* contestants. Software can write subject lines for emails that are opened and read at a higher rate than those written by the wetware of our brains. Big data engines determine much of what we are exposed to online, both the content and the advertisements. It allows New Frontier to convert staggering amounts of raw data in real time to tell the story of what's going on in the cannabis sector and to explain what the best decisions are for investors, policy makers, cannabis companies, and others.

It was big data that allowed Facebook to monetize the incomprehensible amount of information they have about you and your friends and their friends and two billion other people—and then sell it to whoever wants to target you for a message or an ad online. It was big data that enabled the Trump campaign and the Russians to win a seemingly unwinnable election by cost-effectively micro-targeting key persuadable voting groups in a few swing states with messages designed and tested to emotionally resonate with them.

Indeed, a key point about going viral today—either online or in life—is that for the overwhelming majority of us, our goal isn't the near impossible task of going so viral that everyone reads our content or knows our brand. Our goal is to go viral with our target audience. Science fiction writer Neal Stephenson offered a terrific analogy about how much virality is needed to be successful. He was asked a question about his fame or lack of it and replied, "It helps to put this in perspective by likening me to the mayor of Des Moines, Iowa." He continued:

> It's true of both the mayor of Des Moines and of me that, out of the world's population of some six billion people, there are a few hundred thousand who consider us important, and who recognize us by name. In the case of the mayor of Des Moines, that is simply the population of the Des Moines metropolitan area. In my case, it is the approximate number of people who are avid readers of my books. In addition, there might be as many as a million or two who would find my name vaguely familiar if they saw it; the same is probably true of the mayor of Des Moines.

That's probably about where I am, unknown to 99% of Americans, but more viral than I ever imagined. For instance, in March 2009, *Rolling Stone* magazine put me on their list of "100 people who are reinventing America." In December 2015, *Huffington Post* wrote that ClimateProgress "has been the best available source of climate-change news for several years," which was always my primary aim.

My main goal in this book is to help you and your message go more viral than you imagined, so you can achieve your primary aim.

OH BROTHER, WHERE ART THOU?

While I was starting to research and write this book in 2017, my oldest brother, Dave, died unexpectedly. My big-hearted, wise-cracking, science-fiction-loving, photo-snapping, insight-generating, *sui generis* brother was mostly an unsung hero. But in Minneapolis, where he lived, he had a SciFi-comedy show on a local community radio station for decades. So he was viral at least among Twin Cities science fiction fans.

His death and the subsequent memorial ceremony changed the way I think about what it means to go viral. My big brother was a larger-than-life figure to me, of course, but it turns out he touched the lives of everyone he met in that corny way George Bailey does in the movie, *It's a Wonderful Life.* Hearing each eulogy (literally "good speech") and then thinking deeply about the life he lived has been mind-changing and life-changing to me.

The truth about virality is that every single interaction you have with someone, every conversation you have, everything you write online, is a chance to go viral. Each interaction is a chance to make a memorable and emotional connection, and perhaps even a life-changing one—whether it's being the most memorable date for your ultimate mate or the most memorable candidate for that job you always wanted or the most memorable friend, teacher, blogger, tweeter, public speaker, eulogizer or parent.

That's what it means to say something that matters rather than just saying more "blah, blah, blah"—and that's what this book is about.

CHAPTER ONE

How to Be a Winner like Trump without Being a Loser like Trump

An emotional speaker always makes his audience feel with him, even when there is nothing in his arguments; which is why many speakers try to overwhelm their audience by mere noise.

—Aristotle, *Rhetoric*

A little hyperbole never hurts.

—Donald Trump, *The Art of the Deal*, 1987

The president's most authentic moments are when he's lying.

—Former GOP Rep. David Jolly (FL), MSNBC, March 2018

Plato anticipated the results of the 2016 Presidential election more than two millennia ago. Around 380 B.C. the famous Greek philosopher—a student of Socrates and a teacher of Aristotle—wrote a dialogue, *Gorgias*, about one of the first masters of persuasive speech or rhetoric. Plato called rhetoric "the art of winning the soul by discourse," but in the digital age, rhetoric is more aptly called the art of creating content that can go viral, content that is both enticing and memorable, clicky and sticky.

Plato gives Gorgias a speech that dramatized the awesome power of rhetoric, a speech that foreshadowed much of modern American politics. Gorgias explains that "if a rhetorician and a doctor visited any city" in Greece, and had to debate in front of the town leaders, "the doctor would be nowhere, but the man who could speak would be chosen, if he so wished." What he was saying is that a skilled speaker, a master salesman, could persuade any audience that he was more of a doctor than a real doctor.

Cut to 2016. A master salesman who is unqualified to be President persuades just enough people that he should be chosen President over a woman who is highly qualified, but is as emotionally uncompelling and wonky as Gorgias' imaginary doctor.

Or maybe not so imaginary, since Gorgias' own brother was a doctor, while Gorgias was the viral communicator in the family. Gorgias told of seeing patients refuse his brother's medicine or the application of a knife, yet Gorgias was able to convince them to accept the treatment "just by the use of rhetoric."

No wonder a master of viral, figurative speech like Trump can persuade people to do for him what they would not do for so many other candidates—vote. That's why I blogged in March 2016, "If he wins the GOP nomination it will be in large part because of his mastery of rhetoric."

Did you know there is a figure of speech that allows you to lie and exaggerate and say absurdities—"Mexico must pay for the wall" or "the concept of global warming was created by and for the Chinese"—while actually making many people believe you are a genuine and truthful person? Donald Trump does.

How many modern politicians can you name that have been intentionally using key figures of speech for over three decades? In Trump's case one of his favorite figures is hyperbole—or rather "truthful hyperbole" as he labels it in his 1987 bestseller, *The Art of The Deal*:

The final key to the way I promote is bravado. I play to people's fantasies. People may not always think big themselves, but they can still get very excited by those who do. That's why a little hyperbole never hurts. People want to believe that something is the biggest and the greatest and the most spectacular. I call it truthful hyperbole. It's an innocent form of exaggeration—and a very effective form of promotion.

It's an effective form of lying while excusing and rationalizing your lies.

But the hyperbole Trump is using three decades later isn't innocent at all. Why? For one thing, it seems like Trump isn't capable of *not* using hyperbole, of *not* lying to embellish a story. While this may have been a winning strategy during the "anything goes" campaign, it is a losing strategy when you are the commander in chief of the world's most powerful country. Trump's incessant use of hyperbole—such as his infamous and easily disproven exaggeration, "The overall audience was, I think, the biggest ever to watch an inauguration address"—has mainly served to make him an embarrassment, if not a laughingstock.

Also, a key purpose of hyperbole is to express the emotion of anger, as Aristotle explained in his classic work, *Rhetoric*, the first in-depth study of the art. Aristotle notes that hyperboles "show vehemence of character; and this is why angry people use them more than other people."

When Trump makes wildly over-the-top claims—such as he's going to build a wall and make Mexico pay for it—it has no effect on his supporters to point out that this is hyperbolic nonsense. Quite the reverse. Trump's claim moves them emotionally and persuades them precisely because it is hyperbolic nonsense. They are angry, and he's showing that he is angry too—which is vastly more effective than the bland assertions by the professional politicians that they "understand" there is a lot of anger out there, and they have policies to make things better.

Like Gorgias, Trump is a master of narrative and the figures of speech, which are the building blocks of emotionally compelling storytelling. Research shows that stories and content that evoke specific "high-arousal ... emotions"—positive emotions like awe or negative ones like anger or anxiety—are "more viral," as researchers Jonah Berger and Katherine Milkman explained in a 2012 *Journal of Marketing Research* study. Such stories move people to share content.

Trump is a master of going viral because he is a master of using figurative language to arouse strong positive and negative emotions in people. During the campaign, scholars pointed out Trump's use of many different figures of speech beyond hyperbole—far more figures used far more often than any other major candidate. He's been called "a brilliant master of rhetoric" who, as the *Financial Times* put it, has "plundered the figures of classical rhetoric."

Is Trump's use of the figures intentional or simply his natural speaking style after decades of marketing and branding himself?

The answer is, it doesn't matter. Aristotle's key point—and indeed the point of considerable modern social science research—is that regular people talk using the figures of speech. He explains, "This aptness of language is one thing that makes people believe in the truth of your story." Aristotle continues:

> ... *their minds draw the false conclusion that you are to be trusted from the fact that others behave as you do when*

things are as you describe them; and therefore they take your story to be true, whether it is so or not. Besides, an emotional speaker always makes his audience feel with him, even when there is nothing in his arguments; which is why many speakers try to overwhelm their audience by mere noise.

Trump sounds more sincere than his political opponents because he sounds more human. He has "aptness of language." It is a great irony, to use another figure of speech, that transparent hyperbolic lies actually help make people believe in the truth of Trump's stories. The so-called intelligentsia repeatedly mocks Trump for speaking the way most people do—for using simple language, for repeating himself over and over, and for speaking figuratively rather than logically. Yet, masters of rhetoric and the greatest speechmakers have influenced us with these same strategies, from Jesus to Lincoln to our modern day bards and marketing gurus.

Shakespeare and the great rhetoricians of the past, like Gorgias and Cicero, knew and regularly used some two hundred figures of speech. Equally important, they knew which figures expressed which kind of emotion and when to use them to get the desired emotional effect.

"Your language will be appropriate if it expresses emotion and character," explained Aristotle in *Rhetoric*. "To express emotion, you'll employ the language of anger in speaking of outrage; the language of disgust and discrete reluctance to utter a word when speaking of impiety or foulness; the language of exultation for a tale of glory."

Trump loves the rhetorical device of phony reluctance to utter a word or phrase: "She just said a terrible thing. You know what she said? Shout it out because I don't want to say. OK you're not allowed to say and I never expect to hear that from you again. She said—I never expect to hear that from you again—she said he's a pussy.... That's terrible! Terrible."

This figure, apophasis (from the Greek word for "to deny"), emphasizes a point by pretending to deny it, stresses an idea or image by saying you don't want to discuss it, as with Trump's use of "pussy." A favorite of Cicero's—"I will not even mention the fact that you betrayed us in the Roman people by aiding Catiline" (63 BC)—it's also called paralipsis (from the Greek word for "omission"). Apophasis is perhaps the most important "figure of seduction," the term I used in my 2012 book *Language Intelligence* for the figures that are the most duplicitous.

Trump is a master of phony denial. He is more Ciceronian than Cicero himself:

- I was going to say 'dummy' Bush; I won't say it.
  I won't say it.
- I refuse to call Megyn Kelly a bimbo, because that would not be politically correct.
- Unlike others, I never attacked dopey Jon Stewart for his phony last name. Would never do that!
- I promised I would not say that she [Carly Fiornia] ran Hewlett-Packard into the ground, that she laid off tens of thousands of people and she got viciously fired. I said I will not say it, so I will not say it.

You may be thinking, "But Trump was a terrible candidate, widely despised and viewed as unqualified, so what value were all these language skills?" Indeed he was inarguably a terrible candidate in many respects, one of the most unpopular ever to run for the office. But a Presidential election is an extended debate and popularity contest between individuals. Trump didn't have to prove he'd be a great Republican nominee for President, only that he was better than the alternatives (by a plurality of votes). And once he had the GOP nomination, Trump didn't have to prove that he was a good choice to be President to a majority of voters. He just had to persuade enough people in the right states that he was a better choice than Clinton—or, depending on the target audience, that they were both such poor choices a lukewarm Clinton voter should vote for a third-party or not vote at all.

After all, when Gorgias said he could persuade a city Assembly that he should be chosen as doctor over a real doctor, he was commenting not only on his mastery of figurative speaking but also on the literal-mindedness of scientifically-inclined people. That would be an apt description of Hillary Clinton, who, as *Politico* reported in July 2016, "is known for taking a draft of a speech and changing it some indelible way to make it more literal and less readable." *Politico* reveals one campaign joke was that she'd turn the figurative and memorable slogan, "If you see something, say something," into the more literal-minded (and hence easily forgotten), "If you see something, alert the proper authorities."

That is funny—but also fatal. Clinton is part of a long line of wonky literalists the Democrats keep nominating, who inevitably disappoint supporters when they under-perform, especially when they are running against a vastly superior communicator.

An election is not some abstract logical exercise in determining the "truth" of who is most qualified or who has the best policies. Most voters, especially those who aren't hard-core partisans, do not have the time or interest to assess which policies are superior for various complex social problems, such as health care or poverty or terrorism or the opioid epidemic. And even if they did, they'd still have to figure out whether they believe the candidates are even going to seriously try to keep their promises, and if so, will they actually be skilled enough to put those policies in place. That's a whole lot of deliberative thinking, a whole lot of metabolic energy, and a whole lot of time to invest. Again, humans developed mental shortcuts to avoid all of that. The shortcuts allow you to quickly figure out whether someone is "in your tribe" and on your side. But most important, the shortcuts allow you to quickly figure out if people are believable and emotionally compelling, if their words have "the ring of truth" to them. The most codified collection of shortcuts, the most time tested, are stories and their key elements—the figures of speech.

Rhetoric was developed for winning public debates. The word itself comes from the ancient Greek, *rhētorikós*, concerning public speech and *rhétōr*, public speaker. In ancient Athens, all citizens needed to excel at public speaking because every citizen was required by Greek law to speak in his own behalf in court.

As Athens grew in size in the fifth and fourth century BC, and endeavored to democratize its courts, it moved from trial by magistrate to a trial by jury, a very large jury. But there was no public prosecutor and the person who presided over the trial had "no power of control or instruction," notes George Kennedy in the book, *The Art of Persuasion in Greece*. Your accuser spoke—without any restrictions—for perhaps a half hour and then you did the same. Sometimes there was one opportunity for a rebuttal. After that, a jury of some 400 or 500 decided your fate by majority vote.

"The popular and unprofessional nature of the jury much relaxed the need for logical, relevant treatment of points of law," explained Kennedy, "and increased opportunities for irrelevant, but brilliant digressions and emotional appeal."

Since you were not required to write your own speech,

some litigants hired a *logographos*, a speechwriter, to prepare their defense. Others studied the basics of speechmaking with a professional rhetorician. Those with even fewer means could read one of the early rhetoric handbooks, which, unsurprisingly, were devoted to teaching potential litigants the best tricks to persuade a jury.

Over time, rhetoric was turned into a set of rules by Greeks such as Gorgias and Aristotle. Romans including Cicero built on their system. Rhetoric was raised to perhaps its highest level in English during the Elizabethan era, where it led to the two greatest collections of rhetoric in the English language—the works of Shakespeare and the King James Bible. But the codification started with the Greeks.

Gorgias believed the figures were irresistible and had the power of enchantment: "Sacred incantations sung with words are bearers of pleasure and banishers of pain, for, merging with opinion in the soul, the power of the incantation is wont to beguile it and persuade it and alter it by witchcraft." The Elizabethans certainly viewed the figures that way. One best-selling sixteenth-century handbook, *The Garden of Eloquence*, asserted that rhetoric makes the orator "the emperour of men's minds & affections, and next to the omnipotent God in the power of persuasion."

If rhetoric sounds to you like a two-edged sword, or like The Force in *Star Wars*, where there is very much a dark side, you are not alone. Plato and Aristotle agreed. They both believed rhetoric was dangerous in the wrong hands, that it needed to be tempered by virtue. The figures are powerfully inspirational and motivational—but they can be used to motivate the worst in people, too.

The term *Sophists* originally applied to those who taught rhetoric, and other subjects, for pay. Sophists like Gorgias and Protagoras proudly boasted they could make the weaker cause appear to be the stronger. Hence *sophistry*, the term for disingenuous arguments.

A 21-year-old Cicero described the birth of rhetoric's dark side in his book *De Inventione*: "But when a certain … depraved imitation of virtue … acquired the power of eloquence unaccompanied by any consideration of moral duty, then low cunning supported by talent began to corrupt cities and undermine the lives of men." That's a chillingly accurate description of Shakespeare's Iago and other seducers—including Donald Trump.

Rhetoric works to grab and keep attention, to make ideas and phrases go viral and stick in your head—a key reason modern marketing whizzes and branding experts stuff their advertisements with them. Trump is nothing if not a marketing and branding genius. He is arguably nothing *but* a marketing and branding genius, since he managed to sell enough Americans on the notion that he was somehow a great businessman and dealmaker, when he is neither.

After all, Trump had six bankruptcies, managed to lose money running casinos, lost $916 million in 1995, the only year we have some of his tax returns, and, as *Fortune* explained, "would be richer if he'd have invested in index funds" with the money he inherited rather than in real estate deals.

Moreover, as *USA Today* reported in the summer of 2016, in the last three decades, Trump has been involved in more than 3,500 lawsuits. He appears to be the plaintiff about as often as he is the defendant, turning "to litigation to distance himself from failing projects that relied on the Trump brand to secure investment," as *USA Today* explained. In addition, "he and his companies refuse to pay even relatively small bills" with contractors, explaining in one deposition, "I don't feel that these people did very much, if anything, with respect to this deal."

The bottom line: Trump is not a great dealmaker, he's a great deal breaker. He is excellent at losing money, especially at helping others lose money. That should make us all marvel even more at his ability to persuade so many people to believe in him. No wonder billionaire Michael Bloomberg and so many others have described him as a con man, literally a "confidence man," someone skilled at winning your confidence in order to take advantage of you. That is the dark side of rhetoric.

Of course, being such a terrific con man and deceptive marketer that you can sell yourself to enough people to win the presidency does not mean you are qualified to be President, any more than Gorgias was qualified to be a good doctor. In Trump's case, his time in office has clearly shown that he is uniquely unqualified. "No rhetoric can be better than the character of its orator, and sometimes it seduces him," warned Kennedy. Indeed, one reason to study rhetoric, one reason I wrote this book, is so you won't be so easily seduced by words—including your own.

Even though rhetoric has a dark side when used by amoral people for immoral ends, that doesn't mean persuasive, memorable, and emotionally compelling storytelling isn't a valuable skill. Quite the reverse. In the right hands, it can inspire people and indeed a whole nation to greatness, as we'll see in the next chapter.

CHAPTER TWO

How to Tell a Viral Story: Word of Mouth from Jesus to Lincoln to Oprah

Evidence strongly suggests that humans in all cultures come to cast their own identity in some sort of narrative form. We are inveterate story tellers.

> —Owen Flanagan, *Consciousness Reconsidered,* 1992

One hundred thousand years of human reliance on story has evolutionarily rewired the human brain to be predisposed to think in story terms.

> —Kendall Haven, *Story Proof: The Science Behind the Startling Power of Stories,* 2007

The ABT is the DNA of story.

> —Park Howell, branding expert, host of *The Business of Story* podcast

Standing outside the door, nervously riffling through my notes, I thought this was going to be my toughest speaking assignment ever. It almost became my worst, but I was able to turn it around by asking one question: "What do the stories of Luke Skywalker, Harry Potter, Spider-Man, and Dorothy in *The Wizard of Oz* have in common?" So let's see if I can do a better job explaining the simple secrets of storytelling here.

When my daughter was eight, she and her teacher

invited me to speak to all of the third grade language classes. I thought I knew how tough that would be. I even told my daughter that I thought speaking to 39 third-graders was equal to speaking to about 3000 adults. But how wrong I was! I'd never been heckled by an eight-year-old at any of my other talks.

I did have a three-part game plan. First, I would talk about the figures of speech in some of their favorite songs, which I often did with my daughter—Taylor Swift's use of irony, Lady Gaga's use of extended metaphor, Lin-Manuel Miranda's brilliant use of all of the figures in *Hamilton* and so on. Second, I'd talk about how the same storyline underlines so many of their favorite tales, books, and movies, the so-called "hero's journey" that Joseph Campbell immortalized in his classic book, *The Hero with a Thousand Faces*, which George Lucas used as a basis for the original *Star Wars* trilogy. Stories—especially heroic stories, like Homer's *Iliad* and *Odyssey*, and so many stories in the Bible—are perhaps the first things humans created that went viral. Third, I'd talk about a simple trick they could use to turn their thoughts and words into a compelling narrative, the "And-But-Therefore" technique that the best scriptwriters use—and that the best public speakers use—which scientist and storytelling guru Randy Olson has been championing for years.

My mistake was to start with the figures rather than the stories. I didn't realize until much later, when I was researching this book, that modern neurological studies show that only compelling narratives capture the entire audience's attention and keep their entire brain engrossed. One study, "Speaker–listener neural coupling underlies successful communication," found that telling a compelling story actually lights up the same parts of the brains of both the speaker and the audience.

But when you show people a film of random events happening in a park, different parts of the viewers' brains light up. Their minds wander to different places. Eight-year-olds in a class with a substitute teacher tend to quickly get restless and even heckle. After all, from an early age, my own daughter would heckle me, as I said in the Introduction, saying "blah, blah, blah" at my adult-speak. So, naturally, one of her friends in the front row started heckling me.

Time slowed down for me during this awkward moment—another of our brain's clever ways of making sure we remember the rawest feelings from such mistakes, so we don't make them again. But I finally did remember to ask my favorite fallback question, "What do the stories of Luke Skywalker, Harry Potter, Spider-Man, and Dorothy in *The Wizard of Oz* have in common?"

This question got the kids focused on thinking about and talking about all of their favorite stories, eager to offer their answers, especially after I offered my own: Those four heroes were each raised by their aunt and uncle. The hero's journey is universal because, at its most basic, it is always a quest for identity. Lacking one or both parents, as so many fictional heroes do, makes them instantly sympathetic figures, but, even more important, overtly uncertain of their role in the world and in need of guidance or help from others. These are two key features of the hero's journey, and indeed they are two key features of the journey we all go through.

My favorite answer offered by one of the kids was, "the characters all change." That, indeed, is a cornerstone of the best-known stories today—the protagonist undergoes conflict and is changed by it. And it was the cornerstone of the very first stories that went viral, the heroic journeys of the great epic poems that appear in every culture, as Campbell showed.

THE ABTs OF VIRAL CONTENT AND PUBLIC SPEAKING

Since stories are what consistently go viral, and since they are essential for memorable and persuasive speaking, the key question is, "What is the basic structure of narratives that go viral?" Put another way, what is the structure of narratives where there is conflict that leads to change and other emotionally compelling consequences? More than 200 years ago, German philosophers developed the notion of *thesis*, *antithesis*, and *synthesis* to describe how intellectual change and transformation occur. An idea is posed (thesis), it is met with a reaction or a conflicting idea (antithesis), and the resolution, the outcome, is some synthesis of the two conflicting ideas.

For the purposes of a basic approach to viral writing or speaking, that complex notion was eventually translated by leading screenwriters into using the words *and* and *but* and *therefore*: ABT. The beginning exposition lays out an idea or a situation with some *and*s, the conflict or reaction is introduced with *but*s and the resulting consequences or change are introduced with *therefore* (although in common speech, *so* is much more common and what I generally use).

While it may seem hard to believe that such a simple idea could be so powerful, almost every viral English speech in history makes use of this structure, and indeed, these specific words, as we will see. That includes Jesus, Shakespeare, Lincoln, Martin Luther King, Oprah Winfrey, and even Donald Trump.

As an aside, while I'm focusing on writing and speaking in English in this book, this narrative structure is truly universal. Classic Chinese, Korean and Japanese narratives—and modern day Japanese *manga* comics—

use a four-part structure called *Kishōtenketsu*. Satomi Tsuboko, an English-to-Japanese translator with scientific training pointed this out after translating Olson's book on ABT, *Houston, We Have a Narrative*, into Japanese. She explains:

> In Japanese, there is a word for a good story structure: "ki-sho-ten-ketsu"—literally meaning "introduction, development, turn, and conclusion"—which coincides with ABT (there are an introduction AND a development, BUT there happens a turn, THEREFORE conclusion comes to settle the situation and wraps up everything.

Let's look at a simple rule for how you would use ABT in your writing—the "rule of replacing," as screenwriters Trey Parker and Matt Stone call it. Parker and Stone are most famous as co-creators and lead writers of the long-running TV series, *South Park* (for which they won a combined 10 primetime Emmys) and the monster Broadway smash, *The Book of Mormon*, the "Best Musical" of 2011 (for which they won a combined seven Tonys and two Grammys).

Parker describes the rule this way:

> [I call it] the rule of replacing "ands" with either "buts" or "therefores." And so it's always like: This happens and then this happens and then this happens. Whenever I can go back in the writing and change that to: This happens, therefore this happens, but this happened; whenever you can replace your "ands" with "buts" or "therefores," it makes for better writing.

It's that simple. Take a draft of your writing or speech and replace as many "ands" (or other connecting words, like "or") as you can with a "but" (or another word of conflict or contradiction, like "yet") or a "therefore" (or similar words, like "so").

The person who has been championing this approach beyond just screen-writing is storytelling guru Randy Olson. As Olson describes himself, he has a Ph.D. in Biology AND achieved tenure as a professor of Marine Biology, "BUT then he developed an interest in the mass communication of science, THEREFORE he resigned his professorship, moved to Hollywood and became a filmmaker." I've had the good fortune to get to know Randy over the past decade and even sit in on some of the story-telling training sessions he does for scientists.

His book on the ABT, *Houston, We Have A Narrative: Why Science Needs Story*, is a must-read for those starting out on the journey of becoming a viral communicator, which means a great storyteller. And the ABT is the cornerstone of history's most viral speeches from Jesus to Shakespeare to Lincoln.

Consider perhaps the first truly viral speech of 2018, the one Oprah Winfrey gave after receiving the Cecil B. DeMille award for lifetime achievement at the Golden Globes ceremony January 7. As *The New York Times* chief TV critic, James Poniewozik, wrote the next day, this highly praised, widely reshown inspirational speech "has inspired a mini 'Oprah 2020' boomlet of speculation in political media." He noted "it had the music and lyrics of the kind of acceptance speech that ends with a balloon drop.... But above all, it's a story. And it's a story about stories."

Here are two key excerpts:

Each of us in this room are celebrated because of the stories that we tell, *and* this year we became the story. *But* it's not just a story affecting the entertainment industry.

It's one that transcends any culture, geography, race, religion, politics, or workplace. *So* I want tonight to express gratitude to all the women who have endured years of abuse and assault because they, like my mother, had children to feed and bills to pay and dreams to pursue. They're the women whose names we'll never know....

I've interviewed *and* portrayed people who've withstood some of the ugliest things life can throw at you, *but* the one quality all of them seem to share is an ability to maintain hope for a brighter morning, even during our darkest nights. *So* I want all the girls watching here, now, to know that a new day is on the horizon!

Olson calls this speech an "ABT Tour De Force," on his blog, ScienceNeedsStory.com. He explains that "Oprah has deep narrative intuition, and the leadership skills—at least in communication dynamics—that our system selects for." His blog is one of the few places online that discusses the ABT framework.

Olson credits one of his teachers, screenwriting guru Frank Daniel, with first explaining the core idea in a 1986 speech:

In a dramatic story the pattern usually for the connecting scenes is: "and then," "but," "therefore," "but," and towards the culmination "meanwhile." *If you don't have this "but" and "therefore" connection between the parts, the story becomes linear, monotonous.* Diaries and chronicles are written that way, but not scripts.

Perhaps you remember that great romance story you keep watching again and again, where the couple meet, instantly fall in love, get married, and both live happily ever after. Of course you don't, since no one is interested in that kind of linear, monotonous story. Indeed, the cliché "and they all lived happily ever after" exists precisely because that's the part of the story no one is interested in—the happy, uneventful stuff. In reality, nobody lives a monotonous, happily-ever-after life. We hunger for stories about conflict and consequences and change, because they help us navigate our lives without any maps and manuals.

Except we do have maps and manuals. As I said in the introduction, the best stories are the highest form of pattern matching and analogy precisely because they are the most detailed descriptions of people's behavior, their decisions—and the consequences—in every conceivable situation. So the stories are our maps and manuals, which is why we study our favorite ones to the point we set them to memory and internalize them to the point that they become our intuition.

Three leading cognitive scientists, Alison Gopnik, Andrew Meltzoff and Patricia Kuhl, summarized decades of developmental research in their 1999 book, *The Scientist in the Crib: What Early Learning Tells Us About the Mind*:

> Our brains were designed by evolution to develop story representations from sensory input that accurately approximate real things and experience in the world. These programs give us the same advantages they give our computers: they let us predict what the world will be like and so act on it effectively. They are nature's way of solving the problem of knowledge.

That said, until very recently, no computer program could match the human brain's ability to sift through staggering amounts of information in real time in a novel situation and make a rapid decision about what to do.

Since these stories represent our programming, it's no surprise that the stories and speeches that have gone viral are the ones that provide instruction and inspiration on navigating the world and our lives.

THE BIBLE AND ABT

Consider the most viral speech in all of human history, which has been heard or read an unknowable tens of billions of times by billions of people, in essentially every major language. I am talking about Jesus' "Sermon on the Mount." The Bible is widely considered the best-selling book of all time, with more than six billion published. But long before people were literate—and still today—countless numbers have heard the verses read aloud in church. And in the Bible, the best known and best quoted speech is a sermon Jesus gave to the multitudes from a mountain top, some twenty-five hundred words long, lasting perhaps twelve minutes.

The Sermon on the Mount famously begins with the Beatitudes (non-narrative blessings): "Blessed are the poor in spirit: for theirs is the kingdom of heaven. Blessed are they that mourn: for they shall be comforted. Blessed are the meek: for they shall inherit the earth...." What follows is a masterclass in storytelling with the figures of speech using the ABT structure. Here is just one of the many memorable passages:

> *And* why take ye thought for raiment [clothing]? Consider the lilies of the field, how they grow; they toil not, neither do they spin:
> *And yet* I say unto you, That even Solomon in all his glory was not arrayed like one of these.
> Wherefore, if God so clothe the grass of the field, which today is, and tomorrow is cast into the oven, shall he not much more clothe you, O ye of little faith?

Therefore take no thought, saying, What shall we eat? *or*, What shall we drink? *or*, Wherewithal shall we be clothed?

... *But* seek ye first the kingdom of God, and his righteousness; *and* all these things shall be added unto you. Take *therefore* no thought for the morrow: for the morrow shall take thought for the things of itself. Sufficient unto the day is the evil thereof.

This short viral sermon has a remarkable 29 "buts" and 13 "therefores."

Randy Olson developed an "index of narrative strength" to quickly determine whether your speech—or anyone's speech—is a good one, or if it simply has too many "ands" and not enough "buts," the key word of contradiction that is the "heart and soul of narrative." To get the Index ranking, add up the total number of "buts" in a speech and divide by the total number of "ands." Then multiply that ratio by 100. You typically need a speech of a thousand words or more to get a fair estimate.

Good speeches tend to have an Index of 20 or higher. Olson analyzed the presidential primary debates and speeches of Donald Trump and every time he scored above a 20. Some of his long primary speeches were in the 30s. He averaged 28, higher than Olson has measured for any presidential candidate. That's why he says of Trump, "There has never been a politician with this deep of an intuition for narrative." A similar calculation for Hillary Clinton averaged about 14, yet another reason she failed to connect with so many voters. Significantly, Olson has noticed that when Trump reads someone else's words off of a teleprompter, his narrative strength drops in half, to Clinton's level. Those canned speeches rarely sound like Trump, they are boring, and it's obvious he doesn't believe these words.

Returning to the Bible, with ninety-eight "ands" and twenty-nine "buts," the Sermon on the Mount has an Index of about 30. But the Sermon is not just a narrative masterpiece, it is a rhetorical one. It is stuffed full of the figures of speech, which is why so many of its passages are so memorable, so quotable. But we would expect Jesus to speak this way.

Remember, the Gospel according to John opens with this repetitive, alliterative sentence: "In the beginning was the Word, and the Word was with God, and the Word was God." As brilliant as the translators of the King James Bible were, however, some Greek words are tricky to translate. They used the word *word* here for the original Greek word *logos*, but it can also be translated as language and speech and even narrative. So God chose to speak to humans through the logos.

The word Gospel is derived from the Old English, *godspell* (good story). This meaning of *spel*(l) is narration. Even today, spell can mean "words used as a magical charm or incantation." For many, Gospel carries the implication "God's story," especially when capitalized, since Gospel generally refers to Jesus' story as related in Matthew, Mark, Luke, and John. And so we could translate the opening of John as "*In the beginning was the Story, and the Story was with God, and the Story was God.*"

To believers, the Bible represents God's most eloquent message to his children, Jesus' story was the Gospel, and Jesus himself was the logos—rhetoric made flesh. No surprise, then, that *The Garden of Eloquence*, a best-selling Elizabethan rhetoric handbook, says that using the figures of speech places a "true Orator ... next to the omnipotent God in the power of persuasion."

SHAKESPEARE AND ABT

Now consider perhaps the second most famous speech in the English language, something not from the Bible, but still translated into almost every language, a speech that has been repeated, live, in front of millions of people, and read or seen on TV and film by millions more. This most viral speech in the most viral play by the world's most viral playwright, begins with one of the most viral (and parodied) opening phrases in the English language, which describes the protagonist's major conflict, an elemental human question stated using the shortest and most elemental words possible:

> *To be or not to be,* that is the question
> Whether 'tis nobler in the mind to suffer
> The slings and arrows of outrageous fortune....

The question for Hamlet, at least on the surface, is whether or not to commit suicide, whether or not to keep enduring the suffering, "the slings and arrows," from the whims of fortune and fate. If he were to die, he could metaphorically sleep, "and by a sleep to say we end, The heart-ache and the thousand natural shocks, That flesh is heir to." The melancholy Dane is saying that to be human is to suffer heartache and endless shocks to which death would bring a wished-for ending.

But then Hamlet offers up his own "but" or antithesis statement in the form of a metaphor from the game of lawn bowling, wherein "the rub" is something that blocks or changes the bowl's trajectory:

> To die, to sleep;
> To sleep, perchance to dream—*ay, there's the rub*:
> For in that sleep of death what dreams may come,
> When we have shuffled off this mortal coil,
> Must give us pause....

Death would be a metaphorical sleep, and perhaps a relief from human suffering, he says, BUT we don't know whether it would be better than living.

At the end, Hamlet sums up his thesis one last time, "Who would fardels [burdens] bear, To grunt and sweat under a weary life...." before restating the BUT part, then launching into the T part (where the T used here is "thus"):

> *But* that the dread of something after death,
> The undiscovere'd country, from whose bourn
> No traveller returns, puzzles the will,
> And makes us rather bear those ills we have
> Than fly to others that we know not of?
> *Thus* conscience does make cowards of us all,
> And *thus* the native hue of resolution
> Is sicklied o'er with the pale cast of thought,
> And enterprises of great pitch and moment
> With this regard their currents turn awry
> And lose the name of action.

Yes, death could be a relief from the endless burdens of being human, BUT, he warns, death could be worse, and THEREFORE I won't take action to kill myself. Note that over the course of this timeless speech Hamlet and Shakespeare have generalized it to the entire human condition "conscience does make cowards *of us all.*"

In short, probably the most famous speech in all of literature, whose virality has endured for centuries, follows the classic form for virality—a narrative told in ABT format using the figures of speech.

LINCOLN AND ABT

As one last classic example, let's look at perhaps the greatest and most viral political speech in the English language—

and perhaps the most well-known eulogy ever delivered—by one of the greatest political masters of the figures and of ABT the world has ever seen.

Like "to be or not to be," the Gettysburg Address is about 270 words long, roughly a two-minute speech. Yet both Shakespeare and Lincoln knew that you only need two minutes to make memorable and emotionally compelling remarks—if you know the secret.

Months after the bloody Battle of Gettysburg in July, 1863, President Lincoln was invited to speak by the committee for the November 19 Consecration of the National Cemetery at Gettysburg: "It is the desire that, after the Oration [by Edward Everett], you, as Chief Executive of the nation, formally set apart these grounds to their sacred use by a few appropriate remarks."

But Lincoln wanted to do more than just set apart or dedicate the grounds. He wanted to do more than eulogize the dead. He wanted to rededicate the nation to the initial proposition that all men are created equal and rededicate the war going forward as a fight not just for the Union, but for that very proposition. So Lincoln literally set aside the whole notion of an ordinary dedication (which is to say, Everett's two-hour oration): "But, in a larger sense, we cannot dedicate—we cannot consecrate—we cannot hallow—this ground. The brave men, living and dead, who struggled here, have consecrated it, far above our poor power to add or detract." And he immediately repeats this theme with his characteristic modesty, "The world will little note, nor long remember what we say here, but it can never forget what they did here." Therefore, "It is for us the living, rather, to be dedicated here to the unfinished work which they who fought here have thus far so nobly advanced."

Lincoln doesn't use the word "therefore," but the specific

ABT words themselves are just the scaffolding. As Olson puts it, "if you've built a strong edifice with them, they can be removed and the building will still stand up on its own." What truly makes this 270-word speech so astonishing, so unique, is that Lincoln used an extended metaphor of birth, death, and resurrection to increase the coherence and impact of his brief remarks. From the very beginning, Lincoln made several references to birth, "Fourscore and seven years ago our *fathers brought forth* on this continent a *new* nation, *conceived* in liberty and dedicated to the proposition that all men are *created* equal." He said the Civil War was testing whether "any nation so *conceived* ...can long endure."

Lincoln then moved on to images and words of death, as befit the horrific battlefield in front of him, with phrases such as "*a final resting-place* for those who here *gave their lives*" and "the brave men, living and *dead*" and "these honored *dead*" and "these *dead*."

Finally, he returned to the original metaphor of birth, but with a twist: "We must resolve that this nation under God shall have a *new birth* of freedom, and that government of the people, by the people, for the people *shall not perish* from the earth."

Birth, death, rebirth, and immortality ("shall not perish")—in a place that we will make sacred ("hallow" and "consecrate" and the key repeated word, "dedicate")— is a stunning extended metaphor that turns into a biblical allusion of hope for transcendence even during the worst suffering. The Battle of Gettysburg becomes a symbolic national crucifixion. Winston Churchill termed Lincoln's speech "the ultimate expression of the majesty of Shakespeare's language."

The allusion to the hero's journey of Jesus, often called "the greatest story ever told," may be lost on most of us today, but in Lincoln's day people were deeply steeped in the Bible, so they would understand such allusions. Indeed, today, it's commonly said that Lincoln used the phrase "four score and seven years ago," simply because it was more poetic than saying "87." And no doubt that factored into his decision, since Lincoln was very much a poet at heart who spent hours reading passages from Shakespeare to his personal secretary, John Hay, as well as to the artist F. B. Carpenter, who describes Lincoln reciting a thirty-six-line speech by Hamlet's uncle from memory, "with a feeling and appreciation unsurpassed by anything I ever witnessed upon the stage."

But many in Lincoln's audience would have understood he was making a biblical allusion. Psalm 90 says, "The days of our years are threescore years and ten; and if by reason of strength they be fourscore years, yet is their strength labour and sorrow; for it is soon cut off, and we fly away." So Lincoln was making a biblical reference to the length of our lives by using the phrase "four score."

Even for those who miss the allusion to Jesus, the journey from birth and death to rebirth and immortality may also be one of the shortest summaries of the hero's journey. It's a storyline that has resonated for thousands of years, and more today than ever. Christopher Vogler explains this point in his highly influential 1998 book *The Writer's Journey: Mythic Structure for Writers*, which turns Campbell's work into a handbook for screenwriters:

> At the heart of every story is a confrontation with death. If the Hero doesn't face actual death, then there's the threat of death or symbolic death in the form of a high-stakes game, love affair, or adventure in which the hero may succeed (live) or fail (die).

Heroes show us how to deal with death. They may survive it, proving that death is not so tough. They may die (perhaps only symbolically) and be reborn, proving the death can be transcended. They may die a Hero's death, transcending death by offering up their lives willingly for a cause, an ideal, or a group.

Heroes that seem to die or who are believed to have died are more plentiful than ever—think Harry Potter in his final battle with Voldemort or Luke Skywalker using the last ounce of his life force to save the remaining rebels, including his sister Leia, at the end of *The Last Jedi* or Hamlet when his uncle sends him off to England to be killed or Jimmy Stewart's portrayal of George Bailey in the movie, *It's a Wonderful Life*, who contemplates suicide but instead gets to see what the world would have been like had he never been born at all. Indeed, Lincoln himself has become a mythic hero, in part because he was assassinated, while he lives on forever through his words and in the ideals he came to symbolize.

In olden days, heroes could aspire to live forever in songs, in the epic poems like the *Iliad* or the *Odyssey* or in the great stories of the Bible. That was the ancient version of going viral, and that's why even today we call a person whose heroic deeds are not widely publicized an "unsung hero," as I call my late brother Dave.

REMEMBERING A MOST EXTRAORDINARY DEED

Our family had arranged for my brother Dave's memorial in Washington, DC on the Saturday after Thanksgiving, 2017. But on Thanksgiving Day, the person who was supposed to emcee it was hospitalized, and so my other brother Dan and I had to fill in. This seemed a bit like karma, since my father, the editor of the local newspaper in our hometown of Middletown, New York, had often emceed events, and since my brother Dave had often been a master of ceremonies for Minneapolis science fiction conventions, providing pun-filled retellings of *Star Wars* and other science fiction classics. He had a great sense of humor, just like my father.

Indeed, the words of one of Shakespeare's greatest characters, Falstaff, a literally larger-than-life comic genius, come to mind whenever I think of Dave: "The brain of this foolish-compounded clay, man, is not able to invent anything that tends to laughter more than I invent, or is invented on me. I am not only witty in myself, but the cause that wit is in other men."

But emceeing his memorial meant we had to try to provide it some structure. So I reviewed with Dan and my daughter all of the remembrances—the eulogies, which is to say, the good stories—that had been sent to us from his Minnesota friends, which we interspersed between the stories told at the ceremony. It turns out that Dave's story was not just filled with hilarious stories he had made up and heart-warming stories of how he had touched other people's lives like a real-life George Bailey, but was an actual story—a hero's journey, in its own way, as so many people's are. While my brother was a lot sillier than Jimmy Stewart's classic character, his story is every bit as much about redemption.

My brother Danny started the eulogies with that story, a story he titled, "Dave's most extraordinary deed":

> I think it's fair to say Dave had a tough adolescence and a tough adulthood, as a result of his relationship with our father. Without getting into specifics, Dave, I am sure for much of his life disliked my father and probably despised

him. And I am not sure if they reconciled before Dad died in 1999, but I doubt it. At any rate, before Dave died, he set up a scholarship in my father's honor—and incidentally set up one in my mother's honor—and I believe … that he rose … above any animosity that he had for my father and chose to forgive him.

I was planning to end the eulogies by telling this part of Dave's story, since it was also astonishing and profound to me that he not only forgave my father, but decided to honor him. There's much more to Dave's story, including some incredible foreshadowing. But even though we take it for granted that people's lives fit a story we're familiar with, the fact that they do fit such a story is still an important and defining feature of what it means to be human.

"One's self-concept or self-identity is fashioned by adaptation of plots from one's cultural stock of stories and myths," explained psychology professor Donald Polkinghorne in a 1991 journal article on "Narrative and Self-Concept." In that sense, the narratives that guide our lives, the epic tales and the myths, were the first stories to go viral.

No doubt early humans told countless stories as we developed language over tens of thousands of years, but only some of them kept being passed down generation after generation. It's not a coincidence that so many similar heroic and redemptive narratives are found in so many different cultures, as Campbell relates in *The Hero with a Thousand Faces*. Those were the stories and myths that were so memorable, so emotionally compelling and inspiring that they survived for thousands of years.

But they did more than survive. They rewired our brain and imprinted themselves in our identities. So, consciously or unconsciously, people keep trying to live out those stories, and those who succeeded most famously have their story added to our cultural myths. Indeed, it's the fact that every one of us knows so many unsung heroes on a similar journey that really proves just how viral these stories continue to be.

Short Words Win,
Short Words Sell

Beware as long as thou livest of strange words.
—Julius Caesar, quoted in *The Art of Rhetoric*, 1560

Never use a long word where a short one will do.
—George Orwell, "Politics and the English Language," 1946

I know words, I have the best words. I have the best, but there is no better word than stupid. Right?
—Donald Trump, 2015

Short words win. Short words sell. They are the best words to use if you want to go viral.

The same is true for short phrases. In an era of snappy sound bites and sexy slogans, the pitch must be pithy or the channel will be changed.

But we've been miseducated to think big words are a sign of an intelligent speaker and simple words are a sign of a simple mind. Consider what happened when a 2016 study by researchers at Carnegie Mellon University found that Trump spoke at a sixth-grade level grammatically—and at a fourth-grade level by one measure of word and sentence length. *New York Magazine* responded with a Facebook video captioned, "Donald J. Trump has the grammar of an 11-year-old. That's not opinion. That's research-proven." It went viral with 3.2 million views and over 45,000 shares and reactions—as good snark often does. A *Mashable* column snarked, "Donald Trump might have trouble if he ever appears on [the TV show] *Are you smarter than a fifth grader?*"

But the fact is that more than two-fifths of Americans are barely literate and all politicians—indeed all of us—must be able to talk to them. When GOP strategist Frank Luntz conducted a focus group of twenty-nine current and former Trump supporters in December 2015 for CBS News, one person noted that Trump was "talking to us not like we're stupid."

The notion that short words win is not a modern gloss on rhetoric. It is not even a new idea. "The most ancient English words are of one syllable, so that the more monosyllables that you use, the truer Englishman you shall seem," explained the poet George Gascoigne in 1575. The first thing an orator must do is "utter his mind in plain words," according to *The Art of Rhetoric*, a best-selling book of Shakespeare's day. The author even quotes Julius Caesar, "Beware as long as thou livest of strange words, as thou would eschew great rocks in the sea."

"There is no more important element in the technique of rhetoric than the continual employment of the best possible word," wrote the young Winston Churchill in an insightful 1897 essay, "The Scaffolding of Rhetoric." With our miseducated modern minds, we dismiss rhetoric as flowery language and hundred-dollar words. "The unreflecting often imagine that the effects of oratory are produced by the use of long words," he notes.

But the reverse is true. The best oratory isn't from long words but from shorter ones. Churchill points out that shorter words are "more ancient" and "more ingrained in the national character." So "they appeal with greater force." That's why "all the speeches of great English rhetoricians…display a uniform preference for short, homely words of common usage."

We hear the truth of Churchill's advice in the words that linger with us from all of the world's great speeches:

* Judge not that ye be not judged
* To be or not to be
* Lend me your ears
* Four score and seven years ago
* Blood, toil, tears and sweat
* Ask not what your country can do for you
* I have a dream

The genius of Shakespeare is a genius he brought to us through the use of short words. The average word length in Shakespeare's masterpiece *Hamlet* is 3.99 letters—much shorter than the average word length in modern tweets. When Lady Macbeth's guilty conscience over the murder of old King Duncan drives her to wash her hands over and over again, and to walk and talk in her sleep, she starts with: "Yet here's a spot," and then, "Out, damn't spot! Out, I say! One—two, why then 'tis time to do't." And she ends her speech by saying, "Yet who would have thought the old man to have had so much blood in him?"

The words have power and pathos because they are so short. Shakespeare distilled his art to its very essence.

Short words stick in our minds, which is why they are found in the phrases we remember, that we pick up and repeat, like the pithy Hebrew idioms that have come into common use through the English found in the King James Bible:

* to pour out one's heart
* a man after his own heart
* to lick the dust
* under the sun

* to fall flat on his face
* sour grapes
* to stand in awe
* from time to time
* to put words in his mouth
* the skin of my teeth

The power of short words to become the language we love to hear again and again can also be heard in the songs that touch us the most. Those who would have been poets in the past now become bards of pop music. Their best songs are works of art—works of rhetorical art.

Here are the opening lines of "Like a Rolling Stone," the 1965 Bob Dylan ballad voted the greatest rock 'n' roll song of all time: "Once upon a time you dressed so fine, You threw the bums a dime in your prime, didn't you?" Dylan is a master of rhetorical devices, learned from studying the great poets and lyricists. His desire to improve his language intelligence was so great, he regularly visited the New York Public Library's microfilm room to read newspapers from the 1850s and 1860s. Why? As he explains in his autobiography, "I wasn't so much interested in the issues as intrigued by the language and rhetoric of the times."

Dylan repeats the simple phrase "How does it feel" eight times in the song. Why? To do what rhetoric does best—involve us in the song *emotionally*. In the next chapter, we'll see many examples of the repetition of simple words in the most popular songs.

Successful ads, like successful speeches and songs, also use simple words that are repeated. Modern marketers spend billions every year pushing their products. To make sure their messages move us, companies build their advertising campaigns around time-tested tricks based on decades of research.

Here are a few memorable ad slogans. In every one of them we hear the power of short words to stick in our memories, to become phrases that affect our choices, the products we pull out our wallets for:

* Just do it
* Got milk?
* We bring good things to life
* The King of Beers
* Have it your way
* When it rains it pours
* Where's the beef?
* We love to fly and it shows
* Good to the last drop
* I'd like to buy the world a Coke
* Be all that you can be
* All the news that's fit to print
* It's the real thing
* No more tears
* Can you hear me now?
* The Few. The Proud. The Marines

You can go a long way on short words.

POLITICS AND SHORT WORDS

Politics is where Madison Avenue meets Main Street in a war of words to win the hearts and minds of voters. Again, simple wins.

President Ronald Reagan was called the Great Communicator, even by his political opponents. The root of that greatness was his simple style. In his crucial debate with President Carter in 1980, he decisively defined himself and his style with two memorable phrases made up of simple words that still pack a punch.

At one point, Carter attacked Reagan for his position

on Medicare. Reagan began his sharp reply, "There you go again," as if he, the challenger, were the wise teacher and Carter the callow youth in need of correction. At the end of the debate, Reagan introduced a key question, a rhetorical question, that has since been repeated by countless candidates. He asked the audience to imagine itself at the polls and about to make the key decision. His words are worth repeating at length to hear just how much you can say with short words repeated often:

> I think when you make that decision, it might be well if you would ask yourself, *are you better off than you were four years ago?* Is it easier for you to go and buy things in the stores than it was four years ago? … Do you feel that our security is as safe, that we're as strong as we were four years ago? And if you answer all of those questions yes, why then, I think your choice is very obvious as to whom you will vote for. If you don't agree, if you don't think that this course that we've been on for the last four years is what you would like to see us follow for the next four, then I could suggest another choice that you have. This country doesn't have to be in the shape that it is in.

Carter, who, before the debate, was close in the polls, lost ground steadily after it and was badly defeated by Reagan. But for this debate, and for Reagan's simple words, the election and world history might have been quite different.

President George W. Bush also liked to keep it simple. Michael Gerson, one of his long-time speech writers, told NBC in 2005, "He likes simple declarative sentences." So should we all.

The Democrats, however, have had a love affair with candidates—from Michael Dukakis to John Kerry to Hillary Clinton—who either cannot speak in simple language naturally or lack the discipline to do so in spite of themselves. In a November 2004 story, "How Bush did it," *Newsweek* reported that "when speechwriters wrote in pithy lines, Kerry would cross them out," saying, "It sounds so slogany." He had it half right: pithy lines are slogany, but slogany is what sells.

Simple slogans prevail in politics (and so do people who speak simply): *Speak softly and carry a big stick*; *New Deal*; *It's the economy, stupid*; *No Child Left Behind.* Bill Clinton's administration was always searching for the simple slogans to put on a complex issue: *Don't ask, don't tell*, as a policy for dealing with gays in the military, and *Mend it, don't end it*, as an approach for dealing with affirmative-action. Classic slogans like these—short words combined with figures of speech such as repetition and rhyme—helped Clinton become the first Democrat in sixty years to win two presidential elections.

What could be simpler than Obama's slogan in his winning 2008 campaign: "Yes, we can"?

When pundits are making fun of Trump, they will often quote his line, "I went to an Ivy League school. I'm very highly educated. I know words, I have the best words," since that line not only makes him sound narcissistic, but, ironically, it also makes him sound inarticulate or even stupid at the same time. But Trump's full quote from 2015 tells a slightly different story:

> It is the level of stupidity that is incredible. I'm telling you, I used to use the word "incompetent." Now I just call them "stupid." I went to an Ivy League school. I'm very highly educated. I know words, I have the best words. I have the best, but there is no better word than stupid. Right? There is none, there is none. There's no, there's no, there's no word like that.

Yes, those may be fourth-grade level remarks, but Trump is still making a point his opponents and all speakers would do well to learn from.

Ernest Hemingway's 1953 short novel, *The Old Man and the Sea*, was also written at a fourth-grade level. This was measured by the same Flesch-Kincaid index of readability—based on word and sentence length—that Trump was rated on. A typical passage from the novel reads, "You did not kill the fish only to keep alive and to sell for food, he thought. You killed him for pride and because you are a fisherman. You loved him when he was alive and you loved him after. If you love him, it is not a sin to kill him. Or is it more?"

But Hemingway, too, was criticized for his use of simple language throughout his career. At one point, William Faulkner insulted him by saying, "He has never been known to use a word that might send a reader to the dictionary." Hemingway responded, "Poor Faulkner. Does he really think big emotions come from big words?"

Indeed, in a 1950 *The New Yorker* interview, Hemingway explained his word choice using language that echoed Churchill's:

> I use the oldest words in the English language. People think I'm an ignorant bastard who doesn't know the ten-dollar words. I know the ten-dollar words. There are older and better words which if you arrange them in the proper combination *you make it stick*. Remember, anybody who pulls his erudition or education on you hasn't any.

Hemingway understood that his goal was to tell stories that created "big emotions" and that meant using short words that "make it stick."

The Nobel Prize in Literature for 1954 was awarded to Hemingway "for his mastery of the art of narrative, most recently demonstrated in *The Old Man and the Sea*, and for the influence that he has exerted on contemporary style." The book also won the Pulitzer Prize, became a major bestseller, and brought his celebrity to a new level of virality. Not bad for fourth-grade level writing.

Repeat, Repeat, Repeat: Only Memorable Memes Go Viral

Man ... is the most imitative of living creatures.

—Aristotle, *Poetics*

If human beings suddenly ceased imitating, all forms of culture would vanish. Neurologists remind us frequently that the human brain is an enormous imitating machine.

—René Girard,
Things Hidden Since the Foundation of the World, 1978

There's a simple rule: You say it again, and you say it again, and you say it again, and you say it again, and you say it again, and then again and again and again and again, and about the time that you're absolutely sick of saying it is about the time that your target audience has heard it for the first time.

—Frank Luntz, "The Persuaders," *Frontline*, PBS, 2004

R epetition and imitation are the twin pillars of going viral—they are literally what going viral means. That's why, when evolutionary biologist Richard Dawkins coined the term *meme* in his 1976 book, *The Selfish Gene*, he used the metaphor of a virus: "When you plant a fertile meme in my mind" you are turning the brain "into a vehicle for the meme's propagation in just the way that a virus may parasitize the genetic mechanism of a host cell."

A meme is an idea, behavior or even a video or a phrase that spreads from person to person in a culture, generally by imitation and its sarcastic twin, parody. Think "The ALS Ice Bucket Challenge" or Grumpy Cat or Gangnam Style or #MeToo. In short, it's something that goes super-viral.

Why did Dawkins choose the term *meme*? "We need a name for the new replicator, a noun which conveys the idea of a unit of cultural transmission, or a unit of imitation," he wrote. "*Mimeme* comes from a suitable Greek root, but I want a monosyllable that sounds a bit like 'gene.'" In ancient Greek, *mimeme* means "that which is imitated." It is the root of the word *mime*. Dawkins knew the word *meme* wasn't a perfect choice, so he added, "If it is any consolation, it could alternatively be thought of as being related to 'memory.'"

Embedding your words or ideas into someone's memory is the key to going viral and the key to being persuasive. Your words or ideas must be sticky or else they will become extinct, like most words and ideas do. And to repeat a central point of this book, the Greeks figured out some twenty-five centuries ago that the figures of speech were the memory tricks the ancient bards used to remember their long epic poems and songs—tricks that also made sure the audience remembered them.

But repetition remains the most important memory trick, and that's been understood for millennia, hence the Latin expression *Repetitio mater memoriae*, "Repetition is the mother of memory."

So, the single most important thing you can do to become more memorable and persuasive, besides becoming a master storyteller, is to become a master repeater. Eloquence requires the repetition of words and phrases. Persuasion requires the repetition of slogans, sentences, and ideas.

The marketing industry has spent billions of dollars studying how to get people to remember their product, their catch phrase, their brand. That's a key reason advertising and branding rely so heavily on the figures, especially the figures of repetition, like alliteration, repeating the first letter or sound, as in Bed, Bath & Beyond, Best Buy, Chuckee Cheese, Dunkin Donuts, Golds Gym, Krispy Kreme, and so on. But the most basic form of repetition is simply repeating a word or a phrase. The slogans of the last chapter stick with us not just because they are simple words in advertisements that are aired repeatedly, but because the words themselves are often repeated within a single ad. The Energizer Bunny "keeps going and going and going." Cats sing for their Meow Mix supper, repeating the phrase "Meow, Meow, Meow, Meow" again and again. And we have the impossible-to-forget AFLAC duck, whose mere mention makes one wince and waddle.

Repetition works. Repetition sells. Repetition creates a brand. The world's major brands spend their money on repetition. TV series and their stars embrace catch-phrases that they repeat endlessly until they become viral memes, like "Bazinga," which Sheldon Cooper (Jim Parsons) uses on the monster CBS hit, *The Big Bang Theory*.

Donald Trump himself became famous for such an endlessly repeated catch phrase. Trump hosted *The Apprentice*, "an American reality game show," from 2004 to 2014. At the end of each episode, Trump would say to one of the contestants, "You're fired!" He became as famous for this tag line as for anything else he had ever done, perhaps more so. And he rode that tag line, that brand, and that fame all the way to the White House.

Many studies find that repeated exposure to a statement increases its acceptance as true, even if it is false. One of the earliest studies on this "illusory-truth effect" asked subjects to rate how certain they were that each of 60 statements was true or false. The same subjects were asked to rate a list of statements two weeks later, four weeks later, and then six weeks later. Some statements from the original list were repeated each time, others were not. The study found "For both true and false statements, there was a significant increase in the validity judgments for the repeated statements and no change in the validity judgments for the nonrepeated statements."

But repetition is not intrinsically good or evil, since it works for statements both false and true. Repetition mustn't be shunned by progressives just because it works for tyrannical leaders who seek to divide us. After all, it also worked for great leaders who sought to unite us, like Lincoln and Churchill and Martin Luther King. So, it must be in the toolbox of all people who want their ideas to go viral, especially because repetition works with all audiences, even those who consider themselves the most sophisticated.

Consider a postelection interview Trump gave in November 2016 with the *New York Times* reporters and editors on key issues like climate change. The coverage from the *Times* was surprisingly positive, considering Trump campaigned as a climate science denier who would undermine all domestic and global efforts to preserve a livable climate, including the 2015 Paris Climate Accord, where more than 190 nations unanimously agreed to limit and reduce carbon pollution. Indeed, Trump's transition team for the Environmental Protection Agency was led by a notorious climate science denier.

Yet here was the *Times*' all-important headline, seen by vastly more people than actually read the story: "Trump, in Interview, Moderates Views but Defies Conventions." And here's the crucial first paragraph, by far the most widely read part of any story: "President-elect Donald J. Trump on Tuesday tempered some of his most extreme campaign promises, dropping his vow to jail Hillary Clinton ... and pledging to have an *open mind* about climate change."

In sharp contrast, scientists and journalists who actually read the interview came away with a very different view. The *Washington Post*'s analysis the next day was headlined, "Trump's new interview with the *New York Times* isn't reassuring. It's deeply alarming." Longtime British journalist Leo Hickman tweeted, "Optimism Trump takes climate seriously & has 'open mind' on Paris sh[ou]ld be tempered by reading what he actually said." Even climate science denier Steven Milloy tweeted, "If you read the entire Trump-NYTimes interview, you'll see claims of a Trump shift on climate are #FakeNews." When those who deny science agree on something with those who accept science, it's probably a sure thing.

So why was there such a sharp difference between the interpretation of those who read the interview and those who heard it in person? Why exactly did the *Times* say Trump has an open mind on climate? Because Trump himself said he has an open mind on climate. In fact, he said it six times in the span of a few minutes.

Virtually all of Trump's remarks were very consistent with his climate science denial:

I have a totally *open mind*.... It's a very complex subject. I'm not sure anybody is ever going to really know. I know we have, they say they have science on one side *but* then they also have those horrible emails that were sent between the scientists.... Terrible. Where they got caught, you know, *so* you see that and you say, what's this all about. I absolutely have an *open mind*.

So, Trump "totally" and "absolutely" has an "open mind," but he doubts scientists will ever know the truth about climate change. And he brings up the hacked emails that were stolen from scientists in 2009, which lead to out of context quotes that seemed to make the scientists look bad, but were just a McDonalds filled with nothingburgers, as seven independent inquiries concluded.

As an aside, note that Trump used the ABT narrative with *but* and *so*. Trump is a master of narrative.

Here Trump speaks to a *Times* journalist about climate deniers: "But a lot of smart people disagree with you. I have a very *open mind*. And I'm going to study a lot of the things that happened on it and we're going to look at it very carefully. But I have an *open mind*." It's almost like somebody told him to keep repeating that reassuring mantra after an especially dubious statement, like when he said: "Sometimes I'll say I'm actually an environmentalist and people will smile in some cases, and other people that know me understand that's true. Open mind."

This is a brilliant rhetorical trick. Trump keeps repeating *open mind* not because he has one, but because he wants his listeners to believe he does—no wonder some have called his tricks hypnosis or even "Trumpnosis." The great Greek rhetorician and Sophist, Gorgias, was also said to exert a hypnotic control over his audience.

The part of the interview that most excited the *Times*, and, as a result, so many of their readers, occurred when they asked about the Paris Climate Accord, which Trump repeatedly pledged to abandon during the campaign: "But are you going to take America out of the world's lead of confronting climate change?" Trump replied, "I'm looking at it very closely.... I'll tell you what. I have an open mind to it. We're going to look very carefully."

Yet over the course of 2018, Trump did as he promised repeatedly during the campaign. He staffed his administration with climate science deniers, gutted Environmental Protection Agency rules aimed at protecting our health and the health of our kids, worked to undermine clean energy like solar and wind power, and, just seven months after this interview, he became the only world leader to announce he would withdraw from the Paris Accord.

But in that interview in November 2016, he surrounded his standard anti-scientific talking points with repeated pledges to have an *open mind* about climate change—and the powerful media mavens in that room gave him the positive news coverage he wanted. So in that moment, the meme "Donald Trump has an open mind" went viral. Although messaging in the moment in a persuasive and entertaining fashion is Trump's superpower, it's also his kryptonite, since his constant lying and flip-flopping have destroyed his credibility with all but his most ardent supporters.

Again, that Trump lacks the character to use repetition for a positive purpose doesn't negate the fact that repetition can make you more memorable and influential. A 2007 study on how "A Repetitive Voice Can Sound Like a Chorus" found that hearing someone express an opinion repeatedly leads listeners "to estimate that the opinion is more widespread relative to hearing the same communicator express the same opinion only once."

Here's how Shakespeare's master of rhetorical seduction, Iago in *Othello*, manipulates Roderigo, a Venetian gentleman who desires Desdemona even though she has just eloped with Othello. Iago tells Roderigo that despite Desdemona's marriage, he can still win her over if he gives Iago money to buy things to woo her with. Iago then launches into the astonishing repetition of the phrase "put money in thy purse" (sell your assets to raise money). In fourteen lines he repeats the phrase a half-dozen times. A few lines later, Iago says, "I have told thee often, and I re-tell thee again and again." Roderigo, as expected, gives in: "I am changed: I'll go sell all my land." Years of studying rhetoric in school taught Shakespeare and his audience that repetition works.

Indeed, simply repeating the same thing over and over again is the top strategy of every master persuader—from small children to large advertisers—and thus is the top strategy of successful politicians. Michael Deaver, the Karl Rove of the Reagan presidency, said in 2003 of the Bush White House: "This business of saying the same thing over and over and over again—which to a lot of Washington insiders and pundits is boring—works. That was sort of what we figured out in the Reagan White House. And I think these people do it very, very well."

In January 2005, the *Washington Post* reported the White House messaging strategy "will use Bush's campaign-honed techniques of mass repetition, never deviating from the script and using the politics of the fear to build support." In May of that year, Bush himself admitted, "In my line of work you got to keep repeating things over and over and over again for the truth to sink in, to kind of catapult the propaganda."

The need to fill a twenty-four-hour news cycle and the ever-growing number of media outlets means to get your message out you must repeat it again and again on every outlet. Much of the public is barely paying attention, including key targets of modern presidential campaigns: the occasional voter and the swing voter.

With the mainstream media more of a stenographer than an honest broker, and with the rise of new media that allow campaigns to deliver messages unfiltered (and let consumers grab only the slant of news they like), repeated distortions and smears are as effective as repeated truths. In fact, the recent scientific research on "fake news" finds it can be more effective than actual news—since the distortions can be designed to hit emotional hot buttons, create irony, or ring truer than the truth would.

Even a non-native speaker like Arnold Schwarzenegger learned the art of selling through repetition, whether selling a movie or selling himself. "You have to do more than just go and have a little press conference," the California governor said in 2005. "So the spectacle, showmanship, selling, promoting, marketing, publicizing, all those things are extremely important." And while he learned the value of endless marketing in Hollywood, in the gym he learned the value of endless repetition, as he told the *New York Times* in 2005: "The more often you do something, the better you get. I come from the world of reps. Remember that. It is all reps."

In mid-August of 2004, the dog days of the Kerry campaign, as their missteps mounted and their messages miscued, I asked someone close to John Kerry why the campaign didn't pick one message and keep repeating it. "We hit them on something different every day," came the reply. "Besides, most of America is not paying as much attention right now as they will in October." The logic was backwards. When people aren't paying much attention, the only message that can get through is one that is repeated over and over, again and again.

Why do most Democrats seem worse at this repetition business than most Republicans? At one level, as Will Rogers said more than seventy years ago, "I don't belong to any organized party. I'm a Democrat." To the extent that Democrats see themselves as the party of diversity, the rainbow coalition, they don't like to encourage message discipline.

But there's another possible reason. Republicans had become the party of the regular churchgoers, and Bush was famously born-again. Church is one of the few places where rhetoric is glorified and repeated endlessly. Those who read the King James Bible regularly are schooling themselves with the greatest single work of rhetoric ever written. So, it is no accident that a born-again Christian like President Bush might be comfortable repeating his message over and over again.

After all, repetition is at the heart of the Bible, starting with Genesis: "And God said, Let there be light: and there was light. And God saw the light, that it was good." And this structure is repeated verse after verse after verse. God repeats to humans, as we've seen, "In the beginning was the Word, and the Word was with God, and the Word was God.

THE MANY FIGURES OF REPETITION

Repetition has never gone out of style in great speech-making to emphasize key words and ideas, to make them stick in the mind.

Consider one of the most popular figures of repetition: rhyme. The 2000 study, "Birds of a feather flock conjointly (?): rhyme as reason in aphorisms," found that if a phrase or aphorism rhymes then people are more likely to view it as true. People more readily believe the phrase "woes unite foes" describes human behavior accurately than they do "woes unite enemies." Years after the 1995 O. J. Simpson murder case, defense attorney Johnnie Cochran's phrase, "If it doesn't fit, you must acquit," still sticks in the mind. It's a powerful mnemonic that hardwires the evidence the jurors saw in the courtroom—when Simpson tried on the bloodstained "murder gloves," they didn't fit—with the verdict Cochran wanted and ultimately won for his client.

Even simple repetition remains powerfully persuasive.

Repetition is so important to rhetoric that there are four dozen figures of speech describing different kinds of repetition. The different figures have different purposes. For instance, *anaphora* repeats the same words at the beginning of a series of sentences or clauses. The best-selling Elizabethan author John Hoskins noted, "this figure beats upon one thing to cause the quicker feeling in the audience." It worked brilliantly to rally a nation at war in Churchill's famous 1940 speech: "We shall fight in France, we shall fight on the seas and oceans, we shall fight … in the air…. We shall fight on the beaches, we shall fight on the landing grounds, we shall fight in the fields and in the streets, we shall fight in the hills…." These words still resonate eight decades later.

Because of its rousing nature, because it can "awake a sleepy or dull person," as Hoskins explained, this figure can be found in most of the greatest speeches and preachings, from the Sermon on the Mount—Jesus' speech opens with the phrase, "Blessed are …" nine times in nine consecutive lines—to Martin Luther King's 1963 speech, which repeats again and again the stirring phrases "I have a dream" and "Let freedom ring."

The converse figure is *epistrophe*—when many clauses have the same ending. Hoskins explains, "This figure is rather of narration or instruction than motion." In his Gettysburg Address, we can hear Lincoln instruct those present that they must "highly resolve … that government of the people, by the people, for the people shall not perish from the earth."

Not all of the power of repetition can be easily described. After discussing several figures of repetition, the author of the Roman rhetoric text *Rhetorica Ad Herrenium* concludes that repetition possesses "an elegance which the ear can distinguish more easily than words can explain."

Perhaps the most elegant—and certainly one of the most popular—figures of repetition is : words repeated in inverse order. Chiasmus is a great source of aphorisms. Mae West famously said, "It's not the men in my life, it's the life in my men." Ray Bradbury advised writers, "You have to know how to accept rejection and reject acceptance."

A chiasmus is perfect for a rejoinder, for turning an insult back on the person who uttered it. In the 2002 movie *Die Another Day*, James Bond (Pierce Brosnan) says to gadget-guru Q (John Cleese), "You're smarter than you look," to which Q replies, "Better than looking smarter than you are."

Chiasmus has proved irresistible to presidents and their speechwriters. In his first inaugural, JFK had two: "Ask not what your country can do for you—ask what you can do for your country," as noted earlier, and "Let us never negotiate out of fear. But let us never fear to negotiate." And we heard it again in President Bush's post-9/11 speech: "Whether we bring our enemies to justice, or bring justice to our enemies, justice will be done." Orators who remember to use chiasmus will be remembered as orators.

Shakespeare was fond of the figure. In *Twelfth Night* he wrote, "Better a witty fool than a foolish wit." Hamlet offers the following instructions on acting: "Suit the action to the word, the word to the action." Jesus was partial to chiasmus:

* Judge not, that ye be not judged.
* The Sabbath was made for man, and not man for the Sabbath.
* Ye have not chosen me, but I have chosen you.

Chiasmus is divine.

Jesus was the master preacher, the master of rhetoric, able to turn his enemies' words against them. When the Pharisees tried "to catch him in his words," by asking him whether or not it was "lawful to give tribute to Caesar," he replied with a memorably rhetorical phrase, "Render to Caesar the things that are Caesar's, and to God the things that are God's." Thus we have yet another reason to study rhetoric: So people will not be able to catch you in your own words.

WE REMEMBER PEOPLE WITH REPETITION

Since eulogy comes from the ancient Greek, *eu* (good) + *logos* (word, speech, narrative), eulogies are about remembering people with good words and good stories. And since repetition is the most powerful memory device, the best eulogies tend to be filled with repeated words and phrases.

In that most famous of eulogies, the Gettysburg Address, Lincoln weaves the word *dedicate/dedicated* into the fabric of his short speech. He starts by saying our nation was "*dedicated* to the proposition that all men are created equal" and that the Civil war is testing whether a nation "so *dedicated* can long endure." He then switches usage to say those present have come to "*dedicate*" part of the battlefield for those who died so the nation might live. But then says, "we cannot *dedicate*, we cannot consecrate" because the soldiers, living and dead, have already done that. Rather, the living must be "*dedicated*" to the unfinished work the soldiers began, "*dedicated* to the great task" of ensuring this "government of the people, by the people, for the people shall not perish from the Earth." This drumbeat repetition marches the listener toward the lesson Lincoln wants to leave them with, a dedication to the eternal survival of democracy in America.

If you Google "best" or "famous" eulogies, one that pops

up on most every list is Oprah Winfrey's eulogy for the civil rights icon Rosa Parks. She opened with the story of how, as a small child, her father told her that Parks refused to give up her seat on the bus (to a white person), and how, when Winfrey met Parks, she "thanked her ... for myself and for every colored girl, every colored boy, who didn't have heroes who were celebrated. I thanked her then."

Winfrey finishes with a memorably repetitious ending:

> I would not be standing here today nor standing where I stand every day had she not chosen to sit down. I know that. I know that. I know that. I know that, and I honor that. Had she not chosen to say we shall not—we shall not be moved.

> So I thank you again, Sister Rosa, for not only confronting the one white man whose seat you took, not only confronting the bus driver, not only for confronting the law, but for confronting history, a history that for 400 years said that you were not even worthy of a glance, certainly no consideration. I thank you for not moving.

> ... I thank you for acting without concern.... You acted without concern for yourself and made life better for us all. We shall not be moved. I marvel at your will. I celebrate your strength to this day. And I am forever grateful, Sister Rosa, for your courage, your conviction. I owe you to succeed. I will not be moved.

You don't need big words to have a big emotional impact. The best eulogies, the best speeches, have short words with a lot of repetition.

You don't need to be Oprah Winfrey to write a simple and memorable eulogy using repetition. At my brother's memorial, the first eulogy I read, from one of Dave's closest friends in the science fiction community, Sharon Kahn, was exemplary.

"There are so many Daves that I miss—I don't know where to start," she began. "There's Baron Dave, as he liked to be known in the SF community." (Here's where I note that my brother was, as he put it, "a real baron of a fake country," Ladonia.)

"Baron Dave was never the guy in charge of the conventions," she explained, "but he was always there running some essential, or totally non-essential but hilarious, function, making sure everyone was having fun: emceeing, interviewing, directing kazoo bands...." Then she proceeded to list the other Daves:

> Baron Dave was also Shockwave Dave, producing an SF radio show for 27 years.
>
> Then there was Editor Dave, who co-founded the *Bozo Bus Tribune* (our Minicon daily newsletter) and helped me run it for 15 or 20 years.
>
> There was DJ Dave, who loved making music compilations for everybody he knew from his wide-ranging and idiosyncratic music collection.
>
> Uncle Dave was beloved by a couple of generation of fannish kids (not to mention all the toddlers in his apartment building who learned how to make funny noises with their mouths whenever they saw him).
>
> Teacher Dave loved to explain things, and for years was my go-to person for making sense of the latest gratuitous changes to iTunes.
>
> I will miss Contrarian Dave, one of those rare friends who know how to argue passionately about ideas without ever once becoming rancorous or personal about it.
>
> Most of all, I miss My Friend Dave.

My brother Dave was large. Like Walt Whitman, he contained multitudes.

CHAPTER FIVE

Irony: The Viral Twist We Can't Resist from Socrates to Seinfeld

No authentic human life is possible without irony.

—Soren Kierkegaard,
The Concept of Irony, 1841

Indeed, a search on YouTube reveals that a majority of videos on green issues that go viral (that is, are viewed by thousands and even millions of people) employ some element of irony.

—Ekin Pehlivan et al.,
"Viral Irony," *Journal of Public Affairs*, 2013

The irony of CNN having a show called "Reliable Sources" is laughable to begin with, but especially so this week. #fakenews

Donald Trump Jr. tweet, December 10, 2017

It's ironic that a speech containing the line, "The world will little note nor long remember what we say here," became perhaps the most noted and long remembered speech in American history. It's ironic that the President best known for "reality television," serial lying, "professional wrestling," and "alternative facts," repeatedly brands genuine news media outlets as "fake news." It's ironic that one of the greatest TV shows of all time, *Seinfeld*, has so often been called a "show about nothing," when it may be the greatest TV show about irony ever made.

But it's definitely not ironic that irony drives virality, since irony is about what's unexpected and often amusing—and humor and the unexpected are a cornerstone of viral content. Irony has been a defining feature of the great viral stories throughout the ages, including Shakespeare's masterpieces. Indeed, a 2011 Elon University study of "the top 20 viral videos as determined by *Time Magazine*," found that "90% of the videos in the sample contained elements of irony." The study, which was on "Factors that lead videos to become internet phenomena," found "Irony was the variable recorded most frequently in this study."

But it's not just ironic videos that go viral. "Sales of the kitsch Three Wolf Moon T-shirt shot up 2,300% after a spate of ironic reviews went viral," the BBC reported in 2009. Amazon told the BBC the T-shirt had astonishingly become the top-selling clothing item in their clothing store. "We'll take ironic fashion any day," the art director of the T-shirt maker told the BBC. "And we're printing another 400,000 more T-shirts…. It's just a fantastic thing."

A 2017 report, "Memes, Memes Everywhere," analyzing viral memes, including ones spawned by the 2016 election, concluded, "The majority of Internet memes are captioned photos that are intended to be funny, or to publicly ridicule human behavior." If you want to be funny, especially if you want to publicly ridicule human behavior, then you need irony—and sarcasm.

After all, irony, as OxfordDictionaries.com defines it, is "A state of affairs or an event that seems deliberately contrary to what one expects and is often wryly amusing as a result." Sarcasm is "The use of irony to mock or convey contempt." Sarcasm is the kissing cousin of irony. Although, since it comes from the Greek for "flesh tearing," perhaps it is better called the biting cousin of irony.

One reason irony is so sticky in your mind is that irony requires the hearer or reader to *think* more, to activate more brain circuits, in order to understand the connections. Irony is a *trope*, from the Greek for *turn*, since it is a figure of speech that turns or changes the meaning of a word away from its literal meaning. Hyperbole and metaphor are also tropes. Social science research explains why tropes are memorable. As one study of "Figures of Rhetoric in Advertising Language" put it (in muddy jargon that no viral meme writer would use), "Effortfully processed information is more readily retrieved from memory than less effortfully processed information." That is, the more involved you are in decoding a message, the more it sticks.

Irony may well be the trickiest figure to decode—so tricky that the term is widely misused. "We submit that *ironic* might be the most abused word in the English language," the editors at Dictionary.com write. "It's *ironic* that many journalists don't understand when to correctly use *irony*," *Columbia Journalism Review* explained in 2011. They quote the *American Heritage Dictionary*'s usage note: "Sometimes, people misapply ironic, irony, and ironically to events and circumstances that might better be described as simply coincidental or improbable, with no particular lessons about human vanity or presumption."

But if you want to master virality, you must master irony in all its forms. So let's look at a few kinds of irony, starting with the original irony, Socratic irony.

SOCRATIC IRONY

Irony derives from the Greek *eironeia*: dissimulation, the term given to the action and speech of the *eiron*, or "dissembler," a stock character in Greek comedy. The first recorded use is the *Republic* by Plato, where "Socrates himself takes on the role of the eiron" and feigns ignorance as he asks "seemingly innocuous and naïve questions which gradually undermine his interlocutor's case," trapping him "into seeing the truth." Many Greeks did not see the truth as Socrates did—they put him to death—so eiron also carries the sense "sly deceiver" or "hypocritical rascal."

In Shakespeare's *Julius Caesar*, Marc Antony plays the eiron in his famous "Friends, Romans, countrymen" speech when he pretends to praise those who killed Caesar even as he whips up the Roman crowd against them. Antony says: "I am no orator, as Brutus is, But—as you know me all—a plain blunt man." It is a mark of eirons and wily orators that they accuse their opponents of being rhetoricians.

Lincoln, a master of rhetoric, was a "plain homespun" speaker, or so goes the legend, a legend he worked hard to create. In an 1859 autobiographical sketch provided to a Pennsylvania newspaper, Lincoln explained, "Of course when I came of age I did not know much." And after that, "I have not been to school since. The little advance I now have upon this store of education, I have picked up from time to time under the pressure of necessity." The self-consciously rhetorical Churchill once opened an attack on his political opponents saying, "These professional intellectuals who revel in decimals and polysyllables...."

In sum, Socratic irony is the streetwise strategy of the master orator who denies eloquence, claiming to be an ordinary Joe, a plainspoken man of the people.

VERBAL IRONY

A second type of irony is best called verbal irony. The first mention of it in English was in 1502: "yronye ...by the whiche a man sayth one & gyveth to understande the contrarye."

Verbal irony is an essential element for debate, dispute, or rebuke. Using verbal irony is a powerful means of turning your opponents' arguments against them, by revealing a deeper truth that destroys their argument. Using verbal irony you can call your opponent a liar without calling your opponent a "liar." That is what Antony does to Brutus in the Roman Forum.

Brutus, in his speech, persuades the crowd that the assassination was justified because Caesar was too ambitious. In making his case, Brutus used the word "honor" four times. Since Brutus was widely respected for his honor, and since he links the citizens' belief in him to that honor, Antony needs to attack that quality in him, but do so indirectly, since Brutus won the crowd over.

Cleverly, Antony uses the word "honorable" ten times in this one speech, perhaps the most famous eulogy in literature. Antony repeatedly says Brutus is an "honourable man" and that all of the conspirators are "honourable." His irony is increasingly blatant: "When that the poor have cried, Caesar hath wept; Ambition should be made of sterner stuff: Yet Brutus says he was ambitious; And Brutus is an honourable man." With this drumbeat, Antony convinces the crowd that there was no justification for killing Caesar, which in turn means the murder was a *dis*honorable act. For a final knockout punch, Antony reveals the existence of Caesar's will to the citizens, showing them the parchment he describes as the final testament of Caesar's love for them. The citizens beg him to read the will. Antony slyly says:

I have o'ershot myself to tell you of it.
I fear I wrong the honourable men
Whose daggers have stabb'd Caesar; I do fear it.

The crowd is now his. One citizen shouts, "They were traitors," and then spits out, "Honourable men!" This speech is a treatise on verbal irony.

This time-tested rhetorical strategy—turning your opponent's words against him, turning them into an ironic commentary on their character or conclusions—has become one of the primary political strategies of our time.

A front page 2011 *Washington Post* story, "GOP's election battle plan against Obama: Use Obama's own words against him," laid out the Republican battle plan: "The new GOP playbook is designed to take one of Obama's great assets—the power of his oratory—and turn it into a liability." Of course, as the story explains, this is little different from the leaked strategy of the president's team: "A similar in-his-own-words strategy has already been adopted by Obama's campaign and the Democratic National Committee designed to portray GOP front-runner Mitt Romney as a flip-flopper."

Both sides fought the 2016 Presidential election using this strategy. Hillary Clinton ran ad after ad of Donald Trump's quotes demeaning women, including his words from the infamous *Access Hollywood* tape: "Grab 'em by the pussy" [with the last word bleeped out] and "When you're a star, they let you do it. You can do anything." Trump also ran ads using Clinton's words against her, including her comments at a September 2016 speech, "You could put half of Trump's supporters into what I call the basket of deplorables." Both Trump's tape and Clinton's comments became viral memes, but ultimately Clinton's remarks probably ended up more damaging, in part because of Trump's superior messaging strategy and in part because the Russians worked overtime to push Clinton's meme and drown out Trump's gaffe, as I'll discuss in later chapters.

DRAMATIC IRONY

One of the central points of irony—of words that actually mean their opposite—is that sometimes it is intentional and sometimes not. The first two types of irony I have discussed are intentional. Socrates tried to appear harmless when he knew he was anything but. Antony, with his drumbeat repetition: "Brutus is an honorable man," is intentionally ironic and even sarcastic.

A third type of irony, dramatic or situational irony, is the unintentional kind. The person who utters the ironic words or performs the ironic deed is not aware of the irony. The irony is revealed or made obvious by someone else—in a work of fiction, by the author, and in a campaign, by the news media or one's political enemies or late-night comedians.

Politicians and their speechwriters are on an endless quest for words and images of dramatic irony that can discredit their opponents. They are aided and encouraged by journalists trying to find the drama in their personality-driven stories. Words and pictures that are unintentionally ironic clearly have more force, since they appear to reveal a hidden truth about the speaker. Think President George W. Bush on the aircraft carrier with the "Mission Accomplished" banner in the background when, as it turns out, the war had hardly begun. Or John Kerry touting his military record when he could not even defend himself against false verbal attacks in the Swift Boat ads by fellow Vietnam veterans. When John McCain briefly suspended his presidential campaign in the fall of 2008 because of the financial crisis, the Obama campaign turned an effort by McCain to show leadership into a moment that ironically underscored the erratic behavior of their seventy-two-year-old opponent.

Dramatic irony applies to audiences—such as theatergoers or TV watchers—who know (or are told) the significance of words and actions when the characters do not. In drama, the audience often knows or quickly learns that the fate awaiting a character is quite different from what the character believes or says. Another character (or the author) may have told us what the truth is or what is going to happen, or we may see it ourselves. For instance, Shakespeare's Iago tells the audience plainly in several early soliloquies that he is a dangerous liar plotting to destroy Othello and the other major characters. So we hear dramatic irony each time one of those characters calls him *honest Iago* or trusts him. We, the audience, know Iago is dishonest, but Othello and the others don't.

Modern times are awash in irony. Most sitcoms are ironic, and the most popular, like *Seinfeld* and *The Simpsons*, tend to be the most ironic. The wildly popular *The Big Bang Theory*—which for much of its eleven seasons has been the top-rated sitcom, indeed the top-rated TV show of any kind—had a premise that guaranteed wave after wave of irony. It's centered on super smart science nerds, primarily men, who are clueless when it comes to women and social settings. The viewer constantly sees the ironic contrast between their narrow academic brilliance and their broad ignorance about relationships.

The Season 11 opening episode from September 2017 has a scene that is as self-referentially ironic as possible. Nerd-in-chief Dr. Sheldon Cooper (played by Jim Parsons) finally proposes to long-time and long-suffering nerd girlfriend Dr. Amy Farrah Fowler (Mayim Bialik). They go to dinner with a couple of her colleagues, who focus their admiration on her and not him.

"They just kept talking about you, and how great you

are, no matter how many times I brought me up," Sheldon says to Amy afterwards. "It's like having Optimus Prime to dinner and not asking him to turn into a truck." When Amy runs out, Sheldon ends up Skyping the most brilliant man he knows for advice, real-life genius Stephen Hawking, leading to this exchange:

> *Sheldon*: Those people were in the presence of a world-class mind, and all they wanted to talk about was their own nonsense.
>
> *Hawking*: Can you see the irony in that statement? ... How about now? ... How about now? ... I'll wait.

Finally, the world-class mind gets some self-awareness, realizes he wasn't being so smart, and apologizes.

Late-night talk shows have become a locus of irony thanks to perhaps the most overtly ironic show in TV history, *The Daily Show*. For a time, this seminal fake news show on Comedy Central generated countless viral, ironic video clips and had more viewers than most cable news shows. Perhaps that was an inevitable outcome of today's super-cynical, super-hypocritical politics. As host Jon Stewart once said of the Bush Administration, "I really think their foreign policy goal is to spread irony throughout the world."

The irony increased on *The Colbert Report*, a *Daily Show* spinoff on which Stephen Colbert portrayed and satirized a blowhard conservative TV pundit named Stephen Colbert. In its October 2005 premiere, Colbert the pundit coined the term "truthiness," which became so instantly viral that in 2006, *Merriam-Webster* named it "Word of the Year," defining it as "truth that comes from the gut, not books" and "the quality of preferring concepts or facts one wishes to be true, rather than concepts of facts known to be true."

The Colbert Report's type of extreme self-referential irony dates back centuries. For instance, Miguel de Cervantes is both the author and narrator of the early seventeenth century classic, *The Ingenious Nobleman Sir Quixote of La Mancha*. But Cervantes later hands off the role of narrator and author to another "historian," with the disclaimer, "I must only acquaint the reader, that if any objection is to be made as to the veracity of this, it is only that the author is an Arabian, and those of that country are not a little addicted to lying." Take that, truthiness.

In 2015, Colbert became host of CBS's *Late Night* talk show. He took over from David Letterman who, as one *New York Times* columnists wrote, "virtually invented the age of irony, and his self-mocking style has kept him a paragon of cool, even as his competitors have grown younger and his audience older." Ironically, Colbert and his brand of humor struggled in the ratings until Trump was elected—and then mocking Trump's words and actions made Colbert the ratings leader. So many late night comedians began mocking Trump, including other former *Daily Show* correspondents like Samantha Bee and John Oliver, that one 2017 analysis by the Center for Media and Public Affairs at George Mason University calculated Trump was on track to be the most mocked president ever.

But Trump was a reality show star, and reality shows are inherently ironic. After all, reality shows, like "professional" wrestling, have as much to do with reality as *Game of Thrones* does. Trump hosted the "American reality game show" *The Apprentice* for fourteen seasons from 2004 to 2014, half of which were *The Celebrity Apprentice*. At the end of each episode, Trump would famously say to one of the contestants, "You're fired!"

In reality, the show "has nothing to do with business," and Trump doesn't actually fire anyone, as two-time *Celeb-*

rity Apprentice contestant, famed magician Penn Gillette, has explained. In a 2012 *Salon* tell-all where the headline asserts "Donald Trump is a whackjob," we learn Trump "Googles himself, rages at critics and insists he's a good businessman." Gillette explains the full irony of the show:

> No actual business skills are tested. It's not even a real game about fake business. I can tell you the rules of chess. I can't tell you the rules to "The Celebrity Apprentice." No one can tell you the rules of "The Celebrity Apprentice." No one. Donald Trump just does what he wants, which is mostly pontificating to people who are sucking up to him…. Annie Duke, the poker genius, and "TCA" veteran, said to me, "It's a pretend game, about pretend business, where you get pretend fired."

Perhaps the ultimate irony is that President Trump doesn't even like to fire people face-to-face, as we've learned. He fires people by tweet or phone or through the media or has his Chief of Staff do it.

Our greatest movies—whether greatness is defined by popular acclaim or critical acclaim—define modern irony. In *Casablanca*, when Claude Rains shuts down Humphrey Bogart's nightclub, and Bogart asks him, "On what ground?" he famously replies, "I'm shocked, shocked to find that gambling is going on in here!" just before a croupier hands him a pile of money, saying, "Your winnings, sir." Rains says softly, "Oh, thank you very much," and then loudly, "Everybody out at once!" The "shocked, shocked" line, which is a figure of speech (*epizeuxis*: words repeated one after another for special effect), has become a catchphrase for labeling ironic hypocrisy, for telling us when a politician or a person in a position of power is speaking out of "both sides of their mouth."

Few events in the twentieth century rival the sinking of the *Titanic* for irony—try Googling "Titanic" and "irony." So it's no surprise that James Cameron's 1997 movie, *Titanic*, was (until his *Avatar*) the top-grossing movie of all time. Even if the event were not historical, audiences know the dangers of hubris, of early lines such as:

"So this is the ship they say is unsinkable."
"It is unsinkable. God himself couldn't sink this ship."

Hubris—arrogant, prideful overconfidence—has an inevitable outcome, as we know from the Bible: "Pride goeth before destruction, and a haughty spirit before a fall." And if the irony is to be complete, the outcome should be self-inflicted:

"So you've not lit the last four boilers then?"
"No, but we're making excellent time."
"Captain, the press knows the size of *Titanic*, let them marvel at her speed, too. We must give them something new to print. And the maiden voyage of *Titanic* must make headlines!"

Those final lines are classic dramatic irony, where the speaker has one meaning, but the audience gets the twist— the headlines are about an epic disaster.

The story of the rise and fall of the powerful is as archetypal as formulas get. The story is retold in Bob Dylan's classic ballad "Like a Rolling Stone." The first four words tell us this will be a fable with a traditional moral, "*Once upon a time* you dressed so fine, You threw the bums a dime in your prime, didn't you?" Dylan's heroine starts rich and "proud," but soon she is "without a home" and "scrounging" for her next meal.

The irony comes from the central personality-driven

plot line. The protagonist becomes his or her own worst enemy through some tragic flaw like hubris or arrogant overconfidence. That makes the fatal wound self-inflicted, which gives the story dramatic irony, while it keeps his or her personality coherent, which gives the story the ring of truth.

These ironic stories touch us not only because we have read them, heard them or watched them countless times in our lives. But also, we have seen them writ large in real life, the stories of people brought low by the same traits that raised them to the heights, like Richard Nixon or Bill Clinton or Newt Gingrich. And today's reporters are on an endless search for the one word or symbol that sums up a man's life, like the reporter in *Citizen Kane* trying to figure out the meaning of Charles Foster Kane's final utterance—"Rosebud." President George H. W. Bush seemed surprised at how a grocery store scanner worked, which seemed to connect his patrician past with the out-of-touch image challenger Bill Clinton was painting of him. The endless replaying of Howard Dean's screaming exhortation to his supporters following his loss in the 2004 Iowa caucus became his "Rosebud," an ironically revealing moment of truth. For Dean, the passion that had brought him so far had gone too far.

Dramatic irony will become more of a core story element for members of the media who are driven to find dramatic, personality-driven political stories instead of humdrum, policy-driven ones that focus on issues. After all, the favorite ironic storyline of politics—the self-inflicted wound—is the favorite for a good reason. In this plot line, the victims are not victims of circumstances, and thus deserving of our sympathy rather than repeated humiliation. Nor are they victims of some outside enemy, powerful and evil, and thus deserving of our help rather than our mockery. No, they are victims of their own flaws and excesses. They deserved their humiliation—and the media does well to point them out as a lesson to us all.

And this brings us to the last of the four kinds of irony, irony of fate.

IRONY OF FATE: POETIC JUSTICE

The irony underlying poetic justice occurs when a person gets the fate they deserve, typically the very opposite of the one they expect or plan for. It is embodied in the concept of karma, in the popular phrase "what goes around comes around." It is a comeuppance. Poetic justice is essentially the figure of speech turned into a dramatic device, as the Elizabethan rhetoric book *The Garden of Eloquence* explained, the use of verbal irony is "chiefly to reprove by derision."

Poetic justice is "a rational distribution of rewards and punishments that represented the cosmos as designed and controlled by a benign Providence," writes John Andrews, the former director of the Folger Shakespeare Library. So, almost by definition, poetic justice is a core motif in the Bible. When people lie to God or disobey Him or break His commandments, judgment is meted out "by a benign Providence." We see this in all of the great stories, starting with Adam and Eve, and Cain and Abel, through to the very end of the Bible.

Poetic justice of all kinds is extremely common in popular culture. At the most basic level, in the vast majority of TV shows, movies, plays, and books, good triumphs over evil. Good is rewarded, evil is destroyed, criminals are captured, boy gets girl. This theme is so commonplace now that it hardly seems ironic, unless a special twist is added. Indeed, the most ironic form of poetic justice is told in a song by two masters of irony, Gilbert and Sullivan, in their classic comic opera, *Mikado*. In the musical, the Mikado, the powerful and pompous ruler of Japan, describes his vision of poetic justice:

> My object all sublime I shall achieve in time—
> To let the punishment fit the crime, The punishment fit the crime;
> And make each pris'ner pent, Unwillingly represent
> A source of innocent merriment, Of innocent merriment!

This is the chorus, which is repeated five more times. In the verses, Gilbert and Sullivan give us examples of their brand of poetic justice. For instance, society's dull speakers will be forced to "hear sermons from mystical Germans who preach from ten till four."

The repeated phrase "innocent merriment" from the chorus is grounded in a profound insight. We enjoy seeing people get justice in the most fitting fashion. In our unfair world, we yearn to see justice, and the more poetic the better.

As Hamlet put it, "'tis sport to have the enginer" [the maker of engines of war] "hoist with his own petard" [blown into the air by his own bomb]. The nonlethal version of this kind of poetic justice—farcical schemes of sitcom stars blowing up in their faces—has been a staple of classic comedies, such as *The Honeymooners* and *I Love Lucy*, and modern ones, like *The Simpsons*. This source of innocent merriment was perfected in that most successful of modern sitcoms, *Seinfeld*.

Missing the point, critics often described *Seinfeld* as a "show about nothing." Some cultural critics even denounced the show for glamorizing a kind of ironic detachment, when the reverse was true. In the vast majority of episodes, the plot was contrived to ensure that the deceit or trickery or hubristic cleverness employed by the main characters at the start comes back to bite them at the end.

Jerry believes, in one episode, that the breasts of a beautiful woman he started dating, Sidra (Teri Hatcher), must be fake. To uncover the truth he enlists his friend Elaine, who learns they are real when she trips in a sauna and grabs them. The audience knows this plot must inevitably backfire. And it does. Jerry, upon learning the breasts are real, invites Sidra to his apartment, but just seconds before Jerry is going to see the breasts, Sidra sees Elaine and walks out on Jerry, saying, "And by the way, they're real, and they're spectacular." Jerry is not rewarded for his shallowness. He is punished for it, and Elaine says to him, "Just when I think you're the shallowest man I've ever met, you somehow manage to drain a little more out of the pool." The breasts were real, but Jerry was not. He was deceitful. That is irony of fate.

The show's finale in 1998 was the ultimate karmic backlash. Many of the people Jerry and his friends harmed over the years through their selfish and deceitful behavior, including Sidra, return to testify against them. Their "crimes" exposed, they end the show in jail, thus receiving both literal and figurative poetic justice. That's innocent merriment.

Shakespeare metes out harsh poetic justice to most every major character. Brutus decides to murder Caesar because he fears that if Caesar is crowned king, he may become a tyrant. "He would be crown'd: How that might change his nature, there's the question." So the greatest poetic justice that Shakespeare can deliver is to have Brutus' nature change after he kills Caesar and acquires some of Caesar's power. Shakespeare makes clear in the play's second half that Brutus has become like Caesar himself, arrogant and egotistical. Brutus becomes like the person he helped murder, and, soon after, kills himself with the same sword he used to stab Caesar, hoist with his own petard.

That people who acquire power become what they once opposed is another standard ironic plotline, from Orson Welles' *Citizen Kane* and George Orwell's *Animal Farm* to *All the King's Men*. In the first three episodes of the *Star Wars* saga, good Jedi hero Anakin Skywalker transforms into evil Jedi-slayer Darth Vader, the dark father. In ironic dramas, power always corrupts. To the extent that the media is increasingly treating politics as an ironic drama, the story line of corrupting power will inevitably become more commonplace, especially since it has the ring of human truth. In June 2004, when Bill Clinton was asked by Dan Rather on *60 Minutes* why he had had an affair with Monica Lewinsky, he replied, "I think I did something for the worst possible reason—just because I could." In life, as in drama, power does, in fact, corrupt.

The other iconic ironic storyline is the reverse of power transforming good to evil: Love transforms evil to good. This is standard fare in comedies, like *Pretty Woman*, where the love of Julia Roberts, the prostitute with a good heart, transforms Richard Gere from a hard-hearted, job-destroying corporate raider into a soft-hearted, job-rescuing corporation saver. And in episodes Four, Five, and Six of *Star Wars*, we see the transformation of Darth Vader, ally to the evil emperor, back to good Anakin Skywalker, who ultimately destroys the emperor, because of the love of his son, Luke Skywalker. This story line also has power because we've seen it in our own lives. People are transformed every day by love, the love of a good man or woman, of family, of God.

Irony in all of its forms *sells*, both in art and in life, so we will never stop seeing and hearing more of it.

A SUNG HERO DREAMS THE POSSIBLE DREAM

Funerals and memorials are solemn affairs, since we are focused on remembering and honoring the life of a deceased loved one. But most humans have a silly side, and for some their sense of humor is one of their defining qualities. Their humor will be remembered, and they would have wanted it to be remembered. And so we end up with the irony of the funny eulogy.

Indeed, if you Google "best eulogies," you'll find that on most lists is a gem from the legendary comedian, John Cleese, in memory of Graham Chapman, his dear friend and fellow member of the unforgettable comedy troupe, *Monty Python's Flying Circus*. Cleese begins:

> Graham Chapman, co-author of the 'Parrot Sketch,' is no more. He has ceased to be, bereft of life, he rests in peace, he has kicked the bucket, hopped the twig, bit the dust, snuffed it, breathed his last, and gone to meet the Great Head of Light Entertainment in the sky, and I guess that we're all thinking how sad it is that a man of such talent, such capability and kindness, of such intelligence should now be so suddenly spirited away at the age of only forty-eight, before he'd achieved many of the things of which he was capable, and before he'd had enough fun.

> Well, I feel that I should say, "Nonsense. Good riddance to him, the freeloading bastard! I hope he fries." And the reason I think I should say this is, he would never forgive me if I didn't, if I threw away this opportunity to shock you all on his behalf. Anything for him but mindless good taste.

The "Dead Parrot Sketch" is one of Monty Python's most famous and hilarious bits (you can find it online). It is, in its own way, an extended eulogy for a fictional parrot, and the sketch mocks the many euphemisms we have for death. For Cleese, Chapman "was the prince of bad taste. He loved to shock. In fact, Gray, more than anyone I knew, embodied and symbolized all that was most offensive and juvenile in Monty Python." Here's but one memory of Chapman he shares, "I remember writing the undertaker speech with him, and him suggesting the punch line, 'All right, we'll eat her, but if you feel bad about it afterwards, we'll dig a grave and you can throw up into it.'"

Nothing was sacred to Monty Python, which is no doubt one reason my brother Dave loved them so much. The whole family loved Monty Python, but Dave was the one who embodied their spirit the most, especially in the Shockwave Radio Theater skits he wrote for so many years when he lived in Minneapolis.

At his memorial, my brother Dan played an extended clip from one of the most requested of Dave's skits, "The Possible Dream (or The Power of Non-Negative Thinking)," since it captures a side of Dave anyone else's words cannot. The characters are Don Quixote and his sidekick-to-be, Sancho Panza. The scene opens with the sound of horses and the wind:

SANCHO: Whoa there, big boy. Where are you travelling with that armor and lance? You're in a state of total array.

QUIXOTE: My name is Don Quixote, the Man of La Mancha. I'm travelling cognito. I have a bridled passion to become a sung hero.

SANCHO: How very chalant.

QUIXOTE: I'm turbed to hear you say so. I'm something to sneeze at, all right.

SANCHO: Your promptu speech moves me advertantly. I've always wanted to find a person I could hold a candle to. Where are you headed so petuously?

QUIXOTE: I wish to bunk a few myths a told number of times. Chivalry is alive, and if good forces are defatigible it would be skin off my nose.

SANCHO: I can make heads or tails of that. Sir! Your manners are peccable, your hair kempt, your clothing shevelled. My loyalty to my previous employer is swerving and knows bounds. With you I feel capacitated.

QUIXOTE: Then you join me on my quest!

SANCHO: With strong givings....

Dave's favorite figure of speech was *paronomasia*—the pun. But Dave, I believe, did have a bridled passion to become a sung hero. Like so many of us, his possible dream was to go viral on his own terms.

CHAPTER SIX

"Do Not Throw Away Your Shot": Foreshadowing, *Hamilton*, and Virality

Give me the child until he is seven, and I will show you the man.
—Jesuit maxim

We shall not cease from exploration, and the end of all our exploring will be to arrive where we started and know the place for the first time.
—T.S. Elliot, 1942

I'm not throwing away my shot.
I'm not throwing away my shot.
Hey yo, I'm just like my country,
I'm young, scrappy and hungry
And I'm not throwing away my shot
—Alexander Hamilton, early in Lin-Manuel Miranda's musical, foreshadowing how he will die

How can children, and indeed, all of us, watch the same story—or the same storyline—again and again and again, despite knowing the ending?

Within a mere three weeks of my buying the soundtrack to Lin-Manuel Miranda's hip-hop musical masterpiece *Hamilton* in 2016, my nine-year-old daughter had memorized almost all of it. But what's most remarkable is not that Antonia insisted on hearing it over and over again, dozens and dozens of times. After all, she watched *Cinderella* and the first *Harry Potter* movie almost as many times. Nor is it that the *Hamilton* cast album includes every single word sung in a two-and-a-half-hour score—though it is remarkable that she was able to do so given that this fast tempo rap musical has a full 20,500 words. So, as the website FiveThirtyEight.com explained, if it were sung at the tempo of a typical Broadway show, like *Phantom of the Opera* or *Wicked*, then *Hamilton* would run five to six hours long.

No, the most astonishing thing is that some of her friends had also memorized the entire score, and so have many other kids I've met since. It's as if they had all memorized every single line of every single part of Shakespeare's *Julius Caesar*—except nine-year-olds don't do that.

So why is *Hamilton* so compelling to my daughter and countless others of all ages? I asked Antonia why she wanted to listen to it over and over and over again, even when she knew the story word by word, backwards and forwards. Her first answer was, "I like feeling the emotions." Later she said she feels compelled to memorize her favorite songs, to listen again and again until she knows them by heart. But it wasn't until I was writing this book that I realized those answers have the same underlying meaning.

The premise of this book, the Grand Unified Theory of virality, is that from the dawn of language through today, the most viral messages have always been stories told with the figures of speech, which trigger key emotions and stick in the memory. As Kieran Egan explains in *The Educated Mind*, "Oral cultures discovered long ago that ideas and values put into rhythmic story form were more easily remembered and more accurately acted upon." Thus, even today, the most viral videos by far are music videos, which are stories in rhythmic form told with the figures.

Miranda's *Hamilton* is the closest any writer has come to replicating one of the classic epic rhythmic stories about one of the sung heroes of yore, as close as any writer has come to recreating a work of rhetoric as masterful as Shakespeare, but set to music and using modern, accessible language. *Hamilton* is the quintessence of virality, and anyone who is serious about mastering these skills should memorize the whole work.

But I still haven't quite explained the seemingly innate human desire from an early age to see and hear those stories—and heroic tales just like them—again and again. This is where Antonia's first response, "I like feeling the emotions," provides the answer. Even now, Antonia tears up when we get to the part where Hamilton is shot by Burr—and so many other parts. The knowledge of the ending doesn't change how she feels or how anyone watching it feels.

In fact, for those few watching the show the first time who don't know that Alexander Hamilton was killed in a duel by Aaron Burr, Miranda has Burr say to the audience about Hamilton, "And I'm the damn fool that shot him"—at the end of the opening song.

Knowing the ending not only doesn't change Antonia's feelings hearing the story the tenth time—knowing the ending is one of the main reasons she wants to listen to it again and again. Through stories we make sense of the world, we come to understand our role in it, and we create meaning for ourselves. Children have to figure out the answer to even more basic mysteries, such as: why am I feeling all these different emotions and what do they mean?

Stories help answer these questions. "From the beginning, children try to understand the world and self as meaning something by creating stories with plot and temporal sequence," as Valerie Hardcastle, Professor of Psychiatry &

Behavioral Neuroscience, explained in her analysis, "The Development of Self." And emotions tell us which events are meaningful and worth remembering.

So we can never have enough stories. Stories help us give structure to our thoughts and our lives. The best stories, as we've seen, are the highest form of pattern matching and analogy precisely because they are the most detailed descriptions of people's decisions, their behavior with its consequences. And hence, to give us structure, the best stories have a pattern—a beginning, middle, and end that somehow connect. And that brings us back to foreshadowing, the means by which the best stories connect the beginning and the end.

THE ART OF FORESHADOWING

As a theatrical device, the essence of foreshadowing can be found in Anton Chekhov's advice to a novice playwright: "If there is a gun hanging on the wall in the first act, it must fire in the last." Create anticipation and then fulfill the listener's desire.

Foreshadowing is the prequel of repetition—and of irony, as well, for if a person's words or deeds are to become ironic, they must be foreshadowed, they must be hinted at. When a scheme is hatched in the first act of a Shakespeare play or the opening minutes of a sitcom, it must—*must*—backfire in the end.

When a character whose death in a duel is a foregone conclusion keeps repeating "I'm not throwing away my shot," at the start of a play, then he must throw away his shot—firing into the air rather than at Burr—in the final duel that kills him. Indeed, Miranda not only has Hamilton repeat his signature line in his signature song near the start of the musical nearly two dozen times, he repeats it again and again and again throughout the story in various forms, even telling another character, "Do not throw away your shot."

Foreshadowing is related to the figure of speech *ominatio* (Latin for an ominous prophecy or warming). Perhaps the most viral foreshadowing phrase in all of literature occurs in *Julius Caesar*. Shakespeare has a soothsayer famously and futilely warn Caesar, "Beware the Ides of March"—a foreshadowing prophecy that Caesar famously and fatally ignores: "He is a dreamer," shrugs Caesar. "Let us leave him."

But, in stories, it's never wise to ignore dreamers.

I HAVE A DREAM

Perhaps the most remarkable combination of dramatic and rhetorical foreshadowing in a modern public address is the opening lines of Martin Luther King's keynote address at the August 1963 March on Washington for Jobs and Freedom, delivered on the steps of the Lincoln Memorial. The speech is often presented without his introductory sentence, which is unfortunate since it is an essential element of his message.

King began, "I am happy to join with you today in what will go down in *history* as the greatest demonstration for *freedom* in the *history* of our nation." This opening line foreshadows that the focus of the speech will be "freedom," a word that, with its partner "free," King repeats twenty-four times in his ten-minute oration. As we will soon see, it also anticipates his optimistic message.

King uses the word "history" twice in this simple prefatory line, foreshadowing that he will be taking a historical perspective, which he does from the start.

> Five score years ago, a great American, in whose symbolic shadow we stand, signed the Emancipation Proclamation. This momentous decree came as a great beacon light of hope to millions of Negro slaves who had been seared in the flames of withering injustice. It came as a joyous daybreak to end the long night of captivity.

Echoing Lincoln's famous formulation, "fourscore and seven years ago," in the literal shadow of the Lincoln monument, King combines the verbal with the visual to turn Lincoln's two great 1863 acts of communication—the Emancipation Proclamation and Gettysburg Address—into a symbolic foreshadowing of his own remarks one hundred years later. In doubling this historical connection, he underscores what will be his main theme: Emancipation has not yet been realized:

> But one hundred years later, we must face the tragic fact that the Negro is still not free. One hundred years later, the life of the Negro is still sadly crippled by the manacles of segregation and the chains of discrimination. One hundred years later, the Negro lives on a lonely island of poverty in the midst of a vast ocean of material prosperity. One hundred years later, the Negro is still languishing in the corners of American society and finds himself an exile in his own land. So we have come here today to dramatize an appalling condition.

We hear again King's favorite rhetorical device in this speech, anaphora, in the repetition of "one hundred years later" to help him refine the central idea that "the Negro is still not free." King's speech makes the words "Emancipation Proclamation" cruelly ironic: The Negro was proclaimed free, but still is not.

The body of the speech lays out King's nonviolent approach to fulfilling the "quest for freedom" and restates again and again both his dream and his demand for freedom. He says that "in spite of the difficulties and frustrations of the moment, I still have a dream ... a dream deeply rooted in the American dream." An essential goal of the speech is to instill hope, optimism, and faith in the listeners that the dream of freedom will be achieved, to urge with a powerful metaphor that they "not seek to satisfy our thirst for freedom by drinking from the cup of bitterness and hatred." He describes his stirring dreams, which foretell a future without racism, a future of freedom for all. He builds to the climax using the phrase "Let freedom ring" a dozen times and ends with the final repetitions of the key word as he says we can "speed up that day when all of God's children ... will be able to join hands and sing in the words of the old Negro spiritual, 'Free at last! Free at last! Thank God Almighty, we are free at last!'"

Now we see what was foreshadowed in the opening line: "I am happy to join with you today in what will go down in history as the greatest demonstration for freedom in the history of our nation." He is foreshadowing—prophesying—the success of the demonstration and the realization of his dreams.

That King would be a master of rhetoric and foreshadowing is not unexpected since he was, after all, a reverend, a preacher, a student of the Bible. Foreshadowing and prophecy are the foundations upon which the Bible's scaffolding of rhetoric was built—and the power of dreams to foretell the future is a biblical truism. For Christians, the words in the Old Testament foreshadow the coming of the Messiah in the New Testament. The gospels are written to echo the prophecies and promises and proverbs in the Old Testament. If you are a believer, that is because Jesus *is* the Messiah, the fulfillment of the words in the Old Testament.

If you are not a believer, that is because the writers of the New Testament were trying to portray Jesus as the Messiah. Either way, by God's design or man's, the Old Testament foreshadows the New Testament again and again.

Jesus made many prophecies. He foretold events that happen quickly, most famously at the Last Supper when he told the apostles, "One of you will betray me." He foretold events a long time off: "And I say also unto thee, That thou art Peter, and upon this rock I will build my church; and the gates of hell shall not prevail against it." And he foretold events that have not yet come to pass—his return.

Foreshadowing and prophecy are key elements of poetic justice. Consider the story of Joseph. His brothers hated him because their father loved him the most, as evidenced by the gift of the coat of many colors. Joseph dreamt that he and his brothers were collecting stalks of grain, and when his own grain stalk stood up, those of his brothers bowed down before him. "Shalt thou indeed reign over us?" his brothers said. The text goes on, "And they hated him yet the more for his dreams, and for his words." Dreams are classic foreshadowing in the Bible.

One day, when Joseph's brothers saw him in the field, "they said one to another, 'Behold, this dreamer cometh. Come now therefore, and let us slay him, and cast him into some pit ... *and we shall see what will become of his dreams.*'" This is ironic foreshadowing, a favorite device of Shakespeare's and of other great writers. The final line is intended as sarcasm, that the dreams will be dashed in death, but it soon becomes dramatic irony.

Instead of killing him, his brothers sold him into slavery. Joseph ended up in the Egyptian prison, but using his power to interpret dreams, he not only won his freedom but also soon became Pharaoh's right-hand man after predicting that Pharaoh's dream of seven lean cows eating seven fat cows meant there would be seven good harvests followed by seven years of famine. And thus, during the good years, Pharaoh would need to store up the grain. Every prediction Joseph made comes true. Then, during the famine, Jacob sent his sons to Egypt for grain so the family would not starve. Joseph thus gained power over his brothers, whom he put through various trials. But instead of seeking revenge, he reconciled and saved his family from starvation.

This is poetic justice: Joseph's dreams of having power over his brothers came true because they abandoned him, making their words dramatic irony that foreshadowed the end of the story. This is irony of fate.

The enduring power and poignancy of this story can be found in the words on a plaque at the Lorraine Motel, in Memphis, Tennessee, the site of Martin Luther King's assassination (with a slightly different translation than the King James): *Behold, here cometh the dreamer.... Let us slay him ... and we shall see what will become of his dreams.*

WHY FORESHADOWING IS HERE TO STAY

Foreshadowing works for two reasons. First, as described here and in the last chapter, the great stories, from the Greek myths and the Bible to Shakespeare and popular culture, are constructed around irony, around poetic justice that is foreshadowed or forewarned. In *Citizen Kane*, Orson Welles brilliantly starts with Kane's dying word, "Rosebud," and ends with the audience learning that Rosebud is the name of Kane's childhood sled and thus represents his lost innocence and the only time he was truly happy. This leads to the second reason we are enthralled by foreshadowing.

Ultimately, the reason foreshadowing works, and the reason we can expect more of it in popular culture and political coverage is that we like to believe that people's lives have a pattern or consistency. We see that repetition ourselves—the people around us making the same decisions, the same mistakes, over and over again—and if we achieve some wisdom and self-awareness, we realize we repeat ourselves, too. As an example, in *Getting the Love You Want*, one of the basic texts for couples' therapists, Harville Hendrix explains that one of the most reliable indicators for someone falling in love with you is that your negative qualities match those of their opposite sex parent or caregiver. Thus do we tend to repeat the same story as our parents.

Consider an example well-known to social scientists—the "Linda-the-bank-teller problem." Famed cognitive psychologists Dan Kahneman and Amos Tversky gave students the following description of a hypothetical person:

> Linda is 31 years old, single, outspoken, and very bright. She majored in philosophy. As a student, she was deeply concerned with issues of discrimination and social justice, and also participated in anti-nuclear demonstrations.

They had the students rank several statements about Linda on a 1-to-8 scale with 1 being the least probable and 8 being the most probable. Two of the eight statements were as follows:

> Linda is a bank teller. (*T*)
> Linda is a bank teller and is active in the feminist movement. (*T&F*)

From a purely logical or statistical perspective, statement *T* must be more probable than statement *T&F*, since the latter statement presupposes the former is true. And yet when either graduate and medical students with statistical training or Ph.D. candidates in Stanford Business School's Decision Science Program were given this question, more than four-fifths in each group ranked *T&F* as more probable than *T*. They thought it was more likely that Linda was a bank teller *and* a feminist than just a bank teller alone. This result caused a big stir among social scientists, but should not be so surprising. We think in terms of a whole person, and we try to scratch out a consistent story from the facts we get. The original description doesn't match Linda, the bank-teller, that well. But it makes more sense for Linda, the feminist bank teller. Our thinking processes are not purely logical, especially when we are judging other people. As one student remarked after the statistical mistake was pointed out, "I thought you only asked for my opinion."

The Jesuits have a maxim, "Give me the child until he is seven, and I will show you the man." Director Michael Apted built an entire series of films around this idea, that the child foreshadows the man (or woman). He started with *Seven Up*, the 1964 film that began to track the lives of fourteen British youngsters, followed by movies that revisit them every seven years, the most recent being *56 Up* (2012). The films reveal that even seven-year-olds can demonstrate a prophetic view of their lives and there is indeed much of the child in the adult, and vice versa.

Politicians and the media understand that the public believes in foreshadowing. Why else do so many politicians spend so much time telling their personal life story? Why do so many savvy candidates for office spend so much time crafting a story of humble beginnings? Why do so many journalists spend so much time retelling these politicians' stories? Why do so many journalists spend so much time digging for specks of dirt from the distant past, looking for an event or a symbol that casts a shadow over—or perhaps eclipses entirely—a politicians' whole career?

Since the media is increasingly focused on personalities and entertainment, on storytelling and drama, the pressure to find (or invent) foreshadowing will only grow more intense. Why else do so many otherwise smart politicians exaggerate their military service or inflate their resume?

The media bards want an epic song to sing, and the best politicians want to write the lyrics. At an Orlando, Florida rally in March 2005, Barbara Bush shared the story of her son as a stubborn child, concluding, "So, now you can see where the president's tenaciousness comes from—which people also seem to admire so much. It's what you want in a president; it's not what you want in a six-year-old." Give me the child until he is six, and I will show you the president.

Why did Trump, a master of telling stories and branding his perceived enemies, spend so much time questioning Obama's U.S. citizenship and his religion? He wanted to provide foreshadowing for the phony conspiracy theory that Obama is not American, not a true Christian, and therefore "not one of us"—at the same time this attack identified Trump as "one of us." That disgraceful charade also foreshadowed Trump's campaign theme, "Make America Great Again," with its barely concealed racial undertones. The slogan promises a return to some unnamed, imaginary time when America was somehow greater, with the implication that this time was when white males reigned supreme over all other groups.

The foreshadowing in Trump's own life is particularly strong, perhaps because he seems so incapable of change or growth. Even after ascending to the highest position in the land he has not "grown into the job" nor has he ever "pivoted" into a more presidential demeanor, despite the wishful thinking of countless pundits and a great many voters too. The words from his 1987 bestseller, *The Art of The Deal*, are as true today as they were three decades ago. Trump still relies on hyperbole and bravado to sell people fantasies, to excite people "to believe that something is the biggest and the greatest and the most spectacular." His McCarthy-like smearing of entire groups, such as immigrants, was foreshadowed four-and-a-half decades ago when Trump adopted Joe McCarthy's chief counsel, Roy Cohn, as his attorney and then mentor. As the *Washington Post* explained in 2016, "Cohn also showed Trump how to exploit power and instill fear through a simple formula: attack, counterattack and never apologize."

Similarly prophetic are Trump's words on his narcissism, from his 2004 book, *Trump: Think Like a Billionaire*. Trump explains that one "student of successful entrepreneurs," Michael Maccoby, "believes that billionaires like Jeff Bezos, Steve Jobs, and Ted Turner are successful in part because they are narcissists who devote their talent with unrelenting focus to achieving their dreams, *even if it's sometimes at the expense of those around them*" (emphasis added). Trump notes that "Maccoby's book *The Productive Narcissist* makes a convincing argument that narcissism can be a useful quality if you're trying to start a business." Whether you think Trump is a "productive narcissist" or more of a "destructive" one, the point is, Trump has created a self-narrative, a personal myth, to rationalize his narcissism, to rationalize achieving his dreams at the expense of those around him.

THE HERO'S JOURNEY OF REDEMPTION

Foreshadowing works for people for the same reason it works in art: We like straightforward stories and coherent characters. We like a beginning, middle, and end that somehow connect. In his 1991 article, "Narrative and Self-

Concept," psychology professor Donald Polkinghorne put it this way, "we come to know ourselves by discerning a plot that unifies the actions and events of our past with future actions and the events we anticipate."

One plot line makes a disproportionate number of stories in art, from epic poems to epic movies—the hero's journey or monomyth. One reason we see this storyline so often is that so many screenwriters have consciously embraced that plot. We can thank Joseph Campbell's 1949 book, *The Hero with a Thousand Faces*, George Lucas' successful embrace of Campbell's work in the original *Star Wars* movies, and popular books for screenwriters based on Campbell, including Vogler's 1998 book, *The Writer's Journey: Mythic Structure for Writers*, and the *Save the Cat!* series, where Blake Snyder broke Campbell's hero's journey down into a minute-by-minute script template.

But we also see these heroic narratives repeatedly today because they struck a chord with so many people in so many cultures that they went viral for thousands of years. And thus they rewired our brain and imprinted themselves in our identities, as I discussed in Chapter Two—a key reason people keep trying to live out those stories.

My brother Dave played out this story in his own way, as a mostly unsung hero. He left the confines of Middletown, New York, where he had a tough relationship with my father that left him disconnected from the family. He ended up in Minneapolis, where he found a welcoming second home and touched the lives of countless people, particularly in the science fiction community.

At the memorial, my cousin Stephanie explained that she and her daughter visited Dave in the summer of 2016, and were among the last in the family to see him alive. She said Dave told them the simple story of his migration to

Minneapolis, the one he always tells: "He was on his way cross-country and the ride that he got just stopped in Minneapolis, and he just found some roommates, and he stayed."

For monomyth enthusiasts, Middletown would be the "Ordinary World"—Dorothy Gale's Kansas or Luke Skywalker's Tatooine, or Harry Potter's room in his uncle and aunt's house. The Minneapolis SF community would be the "Special World," where Dave's special talents for humor and helping people would flourish, much as Potter's special talents flourish when he entered Hogwarts. And in the end, Dave did rise above his previous anger toward my father to set up a journalism scholarship in my father's honor.

I relate all of this not to mythologize my brother—he had as many flaws as any of us. I'm just trying to explain the remarkable foreshadowing in his story that I relayed in my eulogy:

> It's purely coincidental, but I guess it's more than coincidence, that I was intending to end my remarks the way Danny ended his. We didn't discuss this at all. There's no question David and my father had a challenging relationship. My father had no father for those of you who knew him. Dave as the firstborn got to experience my father not knowing how to be a father, and it is astonishing and profound as Danny said that Dave still—and if you know Dave he carried this anger a very long time—created in the last year the Al Romm Interdisciplinary Journalism Scholarship Fund....
>
> The story of how Dave accidentally ended up in Minneapolis is an amazing story. What often doesn't get mentioned, but Dave knew this to be true at the time, was that my father was born in Minneapolis. I believe a little bit in fate and karma, but at the end of the day, fate is just the choices that we make.

After the memorial, many people asked me about the amazing coincidence that Dave ended up in the place where our father was born. It struck me then that Dave, more than anyone in my immediate family, had kept in touch with my father's relatives for the past two decades. And Dave had traveled to South Africa to meet my grandfather's relatives, since that's where my father's father had moved after he left Minneapolis a few years after my father was born. Indeed, right before he died, Dave traveled to Lithuania, my grandfather's homeland.

"We shall not cease from exploration, and the end of all our exploring will be to arrive where we started and know the place for the first time," as T.S. Elliot wrote in his 1942 poem, "Little Gidding."

CHAPTER SEVEN

Metaphors Are like Warp Drive: The Viral Power of Proto-Stories

The greatest thing by far is to be a master of metaphor....
—Aristotle, *Poetics*

Our ordinary conceptual system, in terms of which we both think and act, is fundamentally metaphorical in nature.
—George Lakoff and Mark Johnson,
Metaphors We Live By, 1980

The human species thinks in metaphors and learns through stories.
—Mary Catherine Bateson, *Peripheral Visions*, 1994

Good metaphors are the Starship Enterprise of figures— they take you from where you are to a completely different place at light speed. But, metaphors can be more like the Millennium Falcon, since as powerful as they are, sometimes they are rickety and don't work. Metaphors are also like a tornado that takes you from Kansas to Oz, a place at once utterly different and yet filled with familiar-looking faces.

At the heart of every story that touches us is a metaphor, something that connects us to the story deeply. We aren't living "a long time ago in a galaxy far, far away" or in a *Star Trek* future centuries from now or in Oz or Hogwarts or Wakanda or Gotham. But we still can identify with and imagine ourselves as Luke or Leia or Han, Kirk or Spock or McCoy, Harry or Hermione or Ron—or Black Panther. We aren't literally superheroes, but we can figuratively aspire to have a hero's journey. As the viral internet meme says, "Always be yourself, unless you can be Batman. Then always be Batman."

Metaphors are so powerful and so universal because they are the most essential of the mental shortcuts that allow us to make sense of the world and quickly figure out the best action in different situations, especially ones we haven't seen before. Because human brains are small and our lifespan was especially short when we were evolving, our brains were "forced to rely on tricks to enlarge memory and speed computation," as E. O. Wilson explained in *Biophilia*. That's why our mind "specializes on analogy and metaphor" for pattern matching.

Pattern matching is most useful when it helps answer this question: How does my current problem or situation resemble another one that I have seen or heard about before? But that's precisely the job of a metaphor. It connects a known situation to an unknown or novel one. How do we make sense of a concept like God? "The Lord is my shepherd" begins Psalm 23. Who is Alexander Hamilton? "I'm just like my country, I'm young, scrappy and hungry. And I'm not throwing away my shot," as his character repeats again and again in his signature song in Lin-Manuel Miranda's viral musical. How can we make sense of Marilyn Monroe's and Princess Diana's tragic deaths? Each was like a "Candle in the Wind," as Elton John sings in his eulogy to Diana (a revision of his eulogy to Monroe), which became one of the best-selling singles in history.

But the true power of a great metaphor is, that like a powerful warp drive, it doesn't just take us on a single trip, but can keep the journey going where no one has gone before. A metaphor can be extended into an allegory or parable, which is really a proto-story. As we've seen, Lincoln used an extended metaphor of birth, death, and resurrection in the Gettysburg Address to turn the story of the country and those who sacrificed their lives to preserve it, into a hero's journey—and, for those familiar with the Bible—specifically Christ's journey. One textbook from Lincoln's day, *Murray's English Exercises*, noted, "An *Allegory* may be regarded as a metaphor continued."

Extended metaphors run throughout the Bible. The Psalms are an extended metaphor menagerie, as are Jesus' parables. For instance, Jesus takes perhaps the Bible's most well-known extended metaphor, Psalm 23's description of God as a shepherd, and extends it further into one of his most famous parables, "I am the good shepherd; I know my sheep and my sheep know me—just as the Father knows me and I know the Father—and I lay down my life for the sheep."

Extended metaphors and similar proto-stories are still powerful. Sociologist Arlie Russell Hochschild makes that clear in her 2016 book, *Strangers in Their Own Land: Anger and Mourning on the American Right*, which she wrote after spending five years getting to know Tea Party activists and Trump supporters in Louisiana. She was trying to understand why so many people in such a poor and highly polluted state voted for politicians who oppose federal government support for poor states and who oppose government rules to clean the environment.

After dozens of interviews she came up with an explanation, a "deep story" underlying their views, "an account of life *as it feels* to them." As she explained in a *Mother Jones* article, their account goes like this:

You are patiently standing in the middle of a long line stretching toward the horizon, where the American Dream awaits. But as you wait, you see people cutting in line ahead of you.

Many of these line-cutters are black—beneficiaries of affirmative action or welfare. Some are career-driven women pushing into jobs they never had before. Then you see immigrants, Mexicans, Somalis, the Syrian refugees yet to come.

As you wait in this unmoving line, you're being asked to feel sorry for them all. You have a good heart. But who is deciding who you should feel compassion for?

Then you see President Barack Hussein Obama waving the line-cutters forward. He's on their side. In fact, isn't he a line-cutter too? How did this fatherless black guy pay for Harvard?

As you wait your turn, Obama is using the money in your pocket to help the line-cutters. He and his liberal backers have removed the shame from taking. The government has become an instrument for redistributing your money to the undeserving. It's not your government anymore; it's theirs.

Hochschild explains she ran the account past her interviewees, and while some made tweaks "all of them agreed it was their story. One man said, 'I live your analogy.' Another said, 'You read my mind.'"

This story, the powerful extended metaphor of the line-cutters, reads like a twisted parable, but my purpose here is not to debunk it. If you listened regularly to the right-wing media for years and years—Fox News, Rush Limbaugh, Breitbart, and other major sources of fake news—you might embrace something like it too. And if this were your extended metaphor, if this were your frame of mind, then you would be receptive to someone who mirrored your anger with his hyperbolic statements, who shared your sense of grievance for the loss of your American Dream with his artfully vague slogan, "Make America Great Again." Indeed, the power of Trump's slogan was that it allowed voters to fill in the details of making America great again with the line-cutter they most resent—without explicitly naming one.

"One of the fundamental findings of cognitive science is that people think in terms of frames and metaphors," wrote linguist George Lakoff in his 2004 best-seller *Don't Think of an Elephant!* "The frames are in the synapses of our brains, physically present in the form of neural circuitry." In recent decades, linguists, cognitive scientists, and others have shown how frames and extended metaphors are at the heart of our thinking about "our most important abstract philosophical concepts, including time, causation, morality, and the mind." Countless books and articles underscore that metaphors and extended metaphors are at the core of human thinking.

WHY METAPHORS MOVE US

So how and why do metaphors move us? Why does one minute of typical speech contain four to six metaphors?

University of Arizona students were asked one of two questions: "How many murders were there last year in Detroit?" or "How many murders were there last year in Michigan?" The median answer the students gave for the city of Detroit was two hundred murders and, for the whole state of Michigan, one hundred. In fact, the rest of Michigan has almost as many murders every year as its most deadly city. But Detroit is a much more dangerous *sounding* place than Michigan. Detroit has become a metaphor for violence and urban decay, and that metaphor framed the answer students gave.

Literal statements are harder to remember than metaphors with the same meaning—even archaic metaphors from Shakespeare. A 1979 study on "Memory for Literary Metaphors," found that lines such as "Your bait of falsehood takes this carp of truth" (by Polonius in *Hamlet*) were better recognized on a later memory test than lines with the same meaning but modern phrasing, such as "Your offering of falsehood takes this gift of truth."

Metaphors make it easier to understand and remember prose. In the 1983 study, "Relation of metaphoric processing to comprehension and memory," people were asked to read short passages on a subject such as how Hitler "committed his people to a course of war." The passages either ended with a literal summary line, "The German people blindly accepted Hitler's dangerous ideas," or a metaphorical one, "The sheep followed the leader over the cliff." Then subjects were tested for their recall of the material. You might expect that the picture was sticky to the brain—but the metaphor was more like a weld. The researchers concluded, "Not only were the concluding metaphors themselves better recalled" than the literal paraphrases, "but there was also an increase in memory for the preceding context."

Metaphors enhance our memories in at least two ways. First, they create another place in the brain for a word or phrase to reside. People remember words better when they have multiple ways to remember them. In particular, metaphors create a visual aid to memory. Take a look at the pictures painted by a few of Shakespeare's most memorable metaphors:

* All the world's a stage
* the dogs of war
* jealousy as the green-eyed monster
* vaulting ambition
* to wear my heart upon my sleeve
* a tower of strength
* who steals my purse steals trash
* music as the food of love

Good talkers far outnumber great speechmakers in part because good talkers tend to be highly verbal people with a strong ability to make remarks that please the ear. They are not necessarily as talented at persuading those who learn better through other senses. To be an effective viral communicator you must be able to persuade all types, not just the highly verbal, but also the highly visual, who make up a large portion of the population. Metaphor is one of the best ways to verbally connect to visual people, and those with high language intelligence are good at painting pictures with words.

Metaphors aid in memory a second way. As evident with the use of irony and other more complex figures of speech, the more involved you are in decoding a message, the more it sticks. Ideally, a metaphor will make you think *and* at the same time create a visual image that connects to an existing memory. That's why metaphors are so common in advertising and brand slogans: Budweiser is "the King of Beers," Chevy Trucks are "Like a Rock," Geico is "so easy a caveman could do it," and "Like a good neighbor, State Farm is there."

THE WEAPONS OF POLITICAL WAR

Given their power, metaphors have naturally become a weapon wielded by all great political speechmakers. Indeed, argument-is-war is an extended metaphor that pervades our language and thinking, one that extends back centuries. The best-selling Elizabethan handbook, *The Garden of Eloquence*, describes the figures of speech as "martial instruments both of defence & invasion." Lincoln explained that the figures of speech used in political warfare "are weapons which hit you, but miss us." Winston Churchill labeled analogy and metaphor "among the most formidable weapons of the rhetorician." For masters of rhetoric, like Lincoln and Churchill, their verbal battles were a kind of warfare because the stakes were so high. As President John F. Kennedy said of Churchill (borrowing from journalist Edward R. Murrow), "He mobilized the English language and sent it into battle" during World War II.

Churchill loved metaphors, and at seventy-one, he gave us his most memorable one, in a March 1946 speech in Fulton, Missouri, that displays his signature "rhymeless, meterless verse":

A shadow has fallen upon the scene
so lately lighted by the Allied victory....
From Stettin in the Baltic
to Trieste in the Adriatic,
an *iron curtain* has descended across the Continent.

A single, well-crafted metaphor, like a well-crafted building, endures.

Kennedy was famous for his mastery of rhetoric. His first inaugural address, written with the help of Ted Sorensen, one of America's best-known speechwriters, is widely considered one of the greatest speeches in the English language. The most viral line is probably the chiasmus, "Ask not what your country can do for you—ask what you can do for your country." But almost as famous is his powerful metaphor,

"Let the word go forth from this time and place, to friend and foe alike, that the torch has been passed to a new generation of Americans...."

A 2005 study on "Presidential Leadership and Charisma," led by psychologist Jeffrey Mio, examined the use of metaphors in the first-term inaugural addresses of three dozen presidents who had been independently rated for charisma. The conclusion: "Charismatic presidents used nearly twice as many metaphors (adjusted for speech length) than non-charismatic presidents." Additionally, when students were asked to read a random group of inaugural addresses and highlight the passages they viewed as most inspiring, "even those presidents who did not appear to be charismatic were still perceived to be more inspiring when they used metaphors."

Extended metaphors are essential to politics for several reasons. First, as we've seen, they are a key to inspiring speeches. Second, since we think with extended metaphors, the best politicians naturally present themselves to fit our metaphors, linking those metaphors to their personal story. When a politician does that, their messages are said to "resonate with the public," touching them personally and emotionally.

Musical resonance is another good metaphor for going viral. The word resonate comes from *resonare*: to sound again, to reverberate, to echo. But it carries the further meaning of amplify and project—like a musical instrument or a concert hall or any cavity designed to amplify and project certain tones. So Trump's racist, anti-immigrant, and misogynist speeches were in tune with the line-cutter parable embraced by much of his target audience. They resonated.

Third, the best way to attack your opponent's positive extended metaphor is to hit back with a negative extended metaphor. Put another way, going viral with voters is the art of creating a persuasive story using figurative language, the art of making—and unmaking—an emotional connection with voters.

The best, most successful political campaigns create two extended metaphors: They paint themselves with a positive one and smear their opponent with a negative one. Losing campaigns either have no extended metaphor or they make one or more gaffes—verbal blunders that allow their opponent to use their words against them to create a fatal negative metaphor.

In 2008, the public wanted change after eight years of Bush. Barack Obama and Hillary Clinton each had a big advantage: They were both powerful visual metaphors for change since neither of them looked like any of the previous presidents. Obama understood this was a change election, and his entire message was built around change, including his simple slogan: "Change we can believe in." In that sense, he had a fully consistent extended metaphor or narrative. In contrast, Hillary Clinton ran as an establishment candidate—the safer choice, the one who could handle a 3:00 a.m. phone call. This fundamental incoherence of message was one of many mistakes that cost her the nomination.

In the general election, Sen. John McCain's campaign suffered from almost the exact same incoherent narrative. On the one hand, he tried to present himself as the steady hand, the war veteran who was more experienced than the young freshman senator from Illinois. But McCain also tried to paint himself as a maverick who would bring change to Washington. His bold gamble to pick Sarah Palin, an unknown governor from Alaska, was meant to highlight his maverick credentials.

You can run as a maverick change agent or you can run

as an experienced, establishment, steady hand. But you can't do both and tell a consistent story. Worse, media interviews made Palin appear as a risky choice to be a heartbeat away from the presidency. When McCain briefly suspended his campaign during the financial crisis, he reinforced the extended metaphor the Obama campaign created for him as being erratic. McCain/Palin became a risky choice.

Sometimes a candidate defines himself or herself in a negative fashion, as Mitt Romney did after winning the Republican presidential primary. Romney was one of the worst communicators in recent memory to win a presidential nomination, much as Hillary Clinton was four years later. *Politico* talked to "thirty different Republican leaders across the country" about Romney, and Executive Editor Jim VandeHei reported on MSNBC's *Morning Joe* June 5, 2012 that "they are so nervous that he'll improvise rhetorically, which got him into a lot of trouble in the primary." They were right to be worried. In a series of off-the-cuff remarks, the former governor and businessman, who was worth a quarter-billion dollars, became the stereotypical out-of-touch rich guy:

- Corporations are people, my friend.
- I like being able to fire people who provide services to me.
- I know what it's like to worry whether you're going to get fired.
- I'm not concerned about the very poor.
- Ann [his wife] drives a couple of Cadillacs, actually.
- I have some great friends who are NASCAR team owners.
- I'm also unemployed.

Each one by itself is a modest gaffe. Together, they were a self-made, self-defeating narrative.

But what wrapped this story in a bow for Obama was when a video leaked on September 17, 2012 of Romney speaking to rich donors at an exclusive fundraiser. Romney said "47% of Americans pay no income tax.... *And so my job is not to worry about those people.* I'll never convince them that they should take personal responsibility and care for their lives."

The video went viral, becoming a defining gaffe. And the "47%" became a metaphor for Romney's lack of concern for half the public. The *Washington Post* columnist Chris Cillizza explained, "Gaffes that matter are those that speak to a larger narrative about a candidate or a doubt/worry that voters already have about that particular candidate." Columnist Michael Kinsley defined the term ironically, "a gaffe is when a politician tells the truth."

Romney learned a painful political lesson: Probably no blunder is greater than one that fits into an elitist narrative that says to a typical voter, "the candidate is not one of us"—or one that dismisses or denigrates a large pool of voters. Hillary Clinton had to relearn the same lesson four years later.

TRUMP VS. CLINTON: HOW VOLDEMORT BEATS HERMIONE

Trump, as we've seen, is a master of figurative speech who connects to his voters emotionally. His use of hyperbole taps into his followers' anger, while avoiding accountability for the vast number of lies that he tells. Nonetheless, his use of repetition, simple language, and key figures like hyperbole and metaphor made his words much more memorable and viral. Even now, you can remember a lot of words, phrases, and even promises from his speeches and tweets. He was going to build a wall and make Mexico pay for it—even if that turns out to be both a metaphor (for getting tough with immigrants) and an outright lie.

Clinton was a classic literal-minded, wonky Democratic candidate who failed to make an emotional connection. She was constantly rewriting her speeches to make them "more literal and less readable," as *Politico* noted in 2016. Can you remember much of what she said during the campaign? Ironically, it was a gaffe in metaphor form that became one of her most memorable and defining moments. During a September 9, 2016 campaign fundraising speech, she said "You know, to just be grossly generalistic, you could put half of Trump's supporters into what I call the basket of deplorables. Right? They're racist, sexist, homophobic, xenophobic—Islamophobic—you name it."

Trump, his supporters, Clinton's opponents, and the media seized on that sweeping insult, repeating it endlessly. "There was one moment when I saw more undecided voters shift to Trump than any other, when it all changed, when voters began to speak differently about their choice," explained Diane Hessan, who tracked undecided voters for Clinton's campaign. "It wasn't FBI Director James Comey, Part One or Part Two; it wasn't Benghazi or the e-mails. No, the conversation shifted the most during the weekend of Sept. 9," after Clinton's "basket of deplorables" gaffe.

The Russian internet trolls also played a big role in repeating and amplifying the "deplorables" line, as we'll see in Chapter Eleven. Hessan compared the gaffe to "Romney's 47 percent"—"proof that, like Romney, Clinton was an out-of-touch rich person who didn't really get it." Her mistake became so potent a metaphor, many of Trump's supporters ultimately took the term "deplorables" as a badge of honor and a brand, wearing T-shirts and hats emblazoned with the word "deplorable."

Why was this gaffe so important to undecideds? Why did it matter so much to people who couldn't decide which candidate they disliked more? Hessan explains what she heard "from scores of undecided voters in swing states":

> They didn't like either candidate. They just wanted to be understood. At the end of the day, they cared less about Trump's temperament and more about whether he "got" them. They were smart…. Trump gave them a voice, and he certainly didn't think they were deplorable.

For voters, nothing trumps emotional connection. As I discussed in Chapter One, the swing voters and undecided voters who aren't hard-core partisans aren't going to devote a lot of mental energy to figuring out which candidate's policies are superior for various complex social problems, like health care. And even if they did, they'd still have to determine if the candidate was committed enough and capable enough to actually deliver their promises.

The simplest shortcut is to bypass all of that analysis and just figure out which candidate was most like them and liked them the most, which candidate was the closest to being in their tribe, which candidate shared their stories and metaphors. By the end of the campaign, that was clearly Trump, and indeed, Trump won the vote among those who disliked both candidates. That was the vital difference in the swing states that decided the election. Whatever those voters disliked about Trump was overcome by the old belief, "the enemy of my enemy is my friend." However strongly people could not stomach Trump, he intensely disliked the same "line-cutters" they did, starting with non-Caucasian immigrants.

The hyperbole "I'm going to build a wall and make Mexico pay for it" matched these voters' anger at immigrants, and "the wall" worked as a metaphorical truth far more potent than a literal one. Trump even had his own powerful and popular extended metaphor he liked to tell about immigrants, one he started telling early on in his campaign and kept repeating, even as President.

"Did anyone ever hear me do 'The Snake' during the campaign?" asked Trump near the end of his February 23, 2018 speech at the Conservative Political Action Conference (CPAC) after a long rant against immigrants. "Because I had five people outside say, 'could you do The Snake?' I said, well, people have heard it. Who hasn't heard 'The Snake'? You should read it anyway. Let's do it anyway. I'll do it. Okay. Should we do it?" This is Trump's standard "phony reluctance" shtick, where he pretends he has to be pushed by his supporters into doing something he always planned. At this point he took out a sheet of paper with the lyrics and continued, "Now, this was a rock 'n' roll song ... but every time I do it, people—and you have to think of this in terms of immigration.... And think of it in terms of immigration and you may love it or you may say, isn't that terrible? Okay. If you say isn't that terrible, who cares?"

Trump then proceeded to read the entire lyrics of this song, which is nearly as long as the Gettysburg Address, albeit less presidential. The song, written and sung in the 1960s by Oscar Brown, Jr., tells the story of "A tenderhearted woman [who] saw a poor half-frozen snake." She takes pity on the snake and takes him in to her home to save him. The chorus is the snake repeating "Take me in, oh tender woman. Take me in, for heaven's sake." After the snake revives, the woman strokes and kisses it, but rather than saying "thank you" to her, "that snake gave her a vicious bite." The song ends:

"I saved you," cried that woman.
"And you've bit me even, why?
You know your bite is poisonous and now I'm going to
die."
"Oh shut up, silly woman," said the reptile with a grin.
"You knew damn well I was a snake before you took me
in."

This emotionally potent parable has multiple meanings, like many parables. Tender, for instance, means to show gentleness, concern or sympathy. But it's other well-known meaning, when referring to food, is easy to chew. The talking, lying snake who tricks a woman is a not very subtle allusion to that most famous talking lying snake who tricks a woman—in the Garden of Eden. The metaphorical connection between a snake and the male sexual organ is as ancient as the Bible.

Of course, in this parable, Trump is casting compassionate Americans in the role of the woman and immigrants in the role of the treacherous snake. But in many respects, Trump is much more like the snake. Trump is the one who denigrated women during the campaign, actually calling Clinton a "nasty woman" at one point. Also, Trump and his team repeatedly use the snake's defense themselves: Voters knew who he was before they voted for him. "Prior to the election it was well known that I have interests in properties all over the world," Trump tweeted on November 12, 2016, responding to questions about his many global conflicts of interest. "Only the crooked media makes this a big deal!" In 2017, when reporters raised the question about the multiple women who accused Trump of sexual abuse, press secretary Sarah Sanders said, "the American people knew this and voted for the president."

Ultimately, the song could serve as a eulogy for the

Republican Party or conservative movement, both of which have sustained deep, self-inflicted wounds from embracing Trump. After Trump's CPAC speech, historian Kevin M. Kruse sent out a tweet that went viral: "Donald Trump is now reading 'The Snake' to a rapt gathering of the conservative movement that has taken him in. RIP, irony."

METAPHORS AND EULOGIES

Eulogies are often metaphorical—not just because they are filled with emotional stories but also because it is hard to adequately express our feelings for a close friend or relative literally. So we use metaphor to describe our connection to the deceased. At the same time, we simply have no literal understanding of death and the hereafter.

Our general unwillingness to confront death is one reason we have so many metaphorical euphemisms for death. These are the very euphemisms that Graham Chapman and *Monty Python's Flying Circus* mocked in the "Dead Parrot" sketch, which John Cleese repeated and amplified in his eulogy for Chapman, "He has ceased to be, bereft of life, he rests in peace, he has kicked the bucket, hopped the twig, bit the dust, snuffed it, breathed his last, and gone to meet the Great Head of Light Entertainment in the sky."

Certainly the eulogies that have gone viral are stuffed with metaphors and similes. Shakespeare has Mark Anthony open his eulogy to his friend Julius Caesar with one of the most famous metaphors in literature, "Friends, Romans, Countrymen, lend me your ears." Lincoln uses an extended metaphor of the hero's journey and the crucifixion to eulogize the fallen at Gettysburg, showing that transcendence is possible even during the worst suffering, to rededicate the listeners to take up their cause—fighting not just for the Union but for the country's founding proposition that all men are created equal. Oprah Winfrey turns Rosa Parks' literal decision to "not be moved" from her seat on the bus into an inspirational extended metaphor for courage and conviction, saying, "We shall not be moved" and "I will not be moved."

At my brother's memorial, many of the eulogies were similarly built around metaphor. For me, as I've said, Dave was like Falstaff. One of Dave's friends from Minneapolis compared him to a magical fountain:

> When I was a child and young teenager, Dave was one of my most cherished adult friends. Some adults were humdrum and some could always find something confusing or intimidating to say, but Dave could somehow always find something funny to say. It was like he was a magical fount of funny factoids, silly sounds, puns and wit. It was a treat whenever I learned he'd be coming over.

Another friend turned the imaginary worlds Dave was always creating into a metaphor of unimaginable loss:

> Dave had a head full of science fiction and strange speculations and wild what-ifs. When we were younger he would sometimes be very insistent on the possible validity of these wild thoughts, but later on he learned that people would be happier to enter into his speculations if he didn't push so hard, and I had some lovely conversations with him about worlds that never existed and probably never could. The world won't be the same without him, not this one and not all the imaginary ones.

Finally, we ended the memorial with that most famous of extended metaphors, one used to provide comfort to the suffering for hundreds and thousands of years:

The Lord is my shepherd; I shall not want. He maketh me to lie down in green pastures:

He leadeth me beside the still waters. He restoreth my soul:

He leadeth me in the paths of righteousness for his name's sake.

Yea, though I walk through the valley of the shadow of death, I will fear no evil:

For thou art with me; Thy rod and thy staff they comfort me.

Thou preparest a table before me in the presence of mine enemies:

Thou anointest my head with oil; my cup runneth over.

Surely goodness and mercy shall follow me all the days of my life:

And I will dwell in the house of the LORD for ever.

It's the Headline, Stupid: Why Big Data and Message Testing Mean Life or Death in the Facebook Era

On the average, five times as many people read the headline as read the body copy.... A change of headline can make a difference of ten to one in sales. I never write fewer than sixteen headlines for a single advertisement.

—David Ogilvy, *Confessions of an Advertising Man*, 1963

Virality is partially driven by physiological arousal. Content that evokes high-arousal positive (awe) or negative (anger or anxiety) emotions is more viral.

—Jonah Berger and Katherine Milkman, "What Makes Online Content Viral," 2012

I understood early that Facebook was how Donald Trump was going to win.... Facebook was the 500-pound gorilla, 80% of the budget kind of thing.... If you imagine the country as the haystack, Facebook is the needle finder.

—Brad Parscale, Trump campaign digital director, *60 Minutes*, October 2017

The subject lines of key emails. The headlines on Facebook ads or other online content. Your tweets. Right now, you are probably *guessing* how they should be worded—and you are almost certainly guessing wrong. As a result, your message needlessly sinks into oblivion.

But today you can easily *know* the best wording to help your message go viral. If you do enough testing, you can even raise a quarter-billion dollars on Facebook and win an upset Presidential election.

There are other ways to boost your chances of going viral on social media. For instance, even if you can't do real-time message testing, you can still use the most time-tested messages, which I did for years and continue to do. You could also go down the path of the dark side of virality, if you're willing to make up fake news stories and set up a systematic operation dedicated to pushing false narratives and helping them go viral with targeted audiences using real-time "big data" analytics. The Trump campaign—with the help of Russia and sites like Steve Bannon's Breitbart—chose this dark path.

Yet you don't have to go Darth Vader online to go viral. You do, however, have to learn from everyone's best practices if you want to give your content the best shot at having a big impact.

Here's a quiz. We tested four different headlines on one of my February 2018 posts for ThinkProgress, whose readers are a mix of 50% Democrats, 35% Independents, and 15% Republicans. One headline was a runaway winner, much clickier and stickier than the others:

- GOP congressman retools Tesla car battery to power his off-grid solar home
- GOP congressman powers his off-grid solar home with a Tesla battery
- This climate-denying congressman just had a great idea for solar-powered homes
- GOP Rep. Massie denies climate science, but loves solar power and Teslas

Can you figure out which one?

WHY TESTING MATTERS

"The most important word in the vocabulary of advertising is TEST." So wrote marketing legend David Ogilvy in his 1963 best-seller, *Confessions of an Advertising Man*. Ogilvy, widely considered "The Father of Advertising," understood that the difference between the right headline and the wrong headline was millions of dollars in sales. Today, the difference between the right headline and the wrong headline online could be millions of views. For me, the right headline can mean getting reposted, retweeted, shared, liked or linked to by social media superheroes like Mark Hamill, Bernie Sanders or Paul Krugman. A well-worded headline—like a well-worded tweet or Facebook post or email—can go viral. Of course, back in Ogilvy's day, testing print headlines and ads was expensive and cumbersome, since he'd have to run different ads on different days or in different publications. But testing is cheap and easy online.

Yet very few people or groups or online publications I talk to test their work. On ThinkProgress, though, we test multiple headlines for every post by having our own readers crowdsource the headline. While we are running a test, readers who come to our site are shown one of the test headlines. Using Chartbeat, a program (and app) from a leading data analytics company, we get real-time analysis of how many people click on each headline, the so-called click through rate (CTR), which has long been the most common measure of the success of online writing, advertising or email campaigns.

But remember, the goal is to be clicky *and* sticky—grabbing your audience's attention *and* keeping it. So for each headline that's clicked on, Chartbeat also tracks how many people stick around 15 seconds or more to actually read a significant portion of the post. Those are called "quality clicks." You may think 15 seconds of reading isn't very long and isn't a demonstration of "quality," but in an era of information overload, 24/7 news, and people reading articles on small smartphone screens, it is. The founding CEO of Chartbeat, Tony Haile, explained on Time.com in 2015:

> Chartbeat looked at deep user behavior across 2 billion visits across the web over the course of a month and found that most people who click don't read. *In fact, a stunning 55% spent fewer than 15 seconds actively on a page.* The stats get a little better if you filter purely for article pages, but even then one in every three visitors spend less than 15 seconds reading articles they land on.

You simply have very little time to grab and keep people's attention.

Returning to the quiz, let me narrow the choices down to two, so you can see that even a small change in wording is the difference between a headline that has a serious chance of going viral and one that does not:

* GOP congressman retools Tesla car battery to power his off-grid solar home
* GOP congressman powers his off-grid solar home with a Tesla battery

One of those headlines had a 5% click-through rate, and of those, only a little more than 60% were quality clicks. So if 20,000 people saw the headline, only 1,000 clicked on it, and only 600 stuck around for 15 seconds or more. That CTR is actually near the high end of the typical article

ThinkProgress posts online, but then the typical posts only occasionally go viral.

The other headline had a 10% CTR—and of those who clicked on that headline, an amazing 92% were quality clicks. If 20,000 people saw the headline, then 2,000 clicked on it and over 1,800 stuck around for 15 seconds or more. These kinds of numbers are associated with posts that have a much greater chance of going viral and a much smaller chance of being a bust. The winning headline was the second one: "GOP congressman powers his off-grid solar home with a Tesla battery." It was written by one of ThinkProgress' headline Houdinis, Patrick Smith. Though I've written thousands of headlines over the years, my original headline was "GOP congressman retools Tesla car battery to power his off-grid solar home." They may look similar, but they aren't the same.

I asked Patrick why his headline did so much better. The answer was that the winning headline gets to the "twist" much sooner. It's unusual that a Republican member of Congress has a solar home, since the GOP leadership have worked to undermine and underfund solar energy, and indeed, all forms of clean energy, whenever they have had a congressional majority. I was too focused on leading with the "news" in the story: A GOP congressman recently released a DIY video showing how he obtained a battery from a used Tesla and retooled it to use in his off-grid solar home.

Again, though, you just don't have a lot of time to grab people. You not only need to have something unusual or ironic or emotionally compelling in your headline, but you also you need to get to the point as quickly and as clearly as possible. The winning headline not only gets to the point fast, but it also tells the story more clearly. Here's a GOP congressman, BUT he has an off-grid solar home, SO he gets a battery from Tesla.

The winning headline pulls off an amazing trick. This headline not only has about *double* the click-through rate of the original headline, but it also has *triple* the number of people spending 15 seconds or more reading the piece. In other words, *the headline itself is still influencing how many people decide to keep reading the post even after they've been reading it for 15 seconds.* So the headline itself can influence the stickiness of the post as much as the content of the post.

Here's another key point: Headlines that are twice as clicky don't get only twice the views. Virality is not a linear effect, where a headline with a CTR of one in ten (10%) merely gets you double the click-throughs (and hence double the page views) of a headline with a CTR of one in 20 (5%). The internet and social media are inherently non-linear because they are networks, and virality is a network effect.

Virality spreads through contagion. So just like a virus, if the transmission rate isn't high enough—if the chances you will catch the virus from someone in a single encounter isn't high enough—the virus will probably fizzle out before having much impact. And just like a virus, the length of time each person stays contagious matters. If someone carrying the virus stays contagious for weeks, the virus is much more likely to create an epidemic than if a carrier is only contagious for a short time. Similarly, if your content is sticky, if it sticks in people's memories or gets on platforms that keep it visible for a long period of time, it is much more likely to go viral.

THE MULTIPLIER EFFECT: WHY HEADLINES REALLY MATTER

Let's take a deeper dive into online virality. The Tesla battery post had about 12,000 direct page views. I've had many posts with ten times that number or more. So a great headline doesn't guarantee hundreds of thousands of people will read your content—it just greatly increases the chances.

But even in the case of the GOP Congressman with off-grid solar, vastly more people saw the headline than the 12,000 who read the story—perhaps a quarter-million people and perhaps a lot more. Just on ThinkProgress, we know that ten times as many people saw the headline as clicked on it. But in the social media era, the headline gets spread far and wide. Between our ThinkProgress and ClimateProgress social media accounts, we send it to a combined following of over one million people on Twitter and two million on Facebook, which then get further retweeted and shared by some of those followers, and some of their followers, and so on.

Also, we need to add in the people who see the headline on content aggregators—sites that repost some or all of content. Our best posts are picked up by Yahoo News, Reddit, Flipboard, Google News, and countless others. For instance, the headline of a popular post picked up by Yahoo will rise close to the top of their front page. If you click on that headline, you generally go to a Yahoo page where the first paragraph of the post is excerpted with a "Read More" link back to ThinkProgress. We know how many people click on that second link, since that shows up in our page view count. But we don't know the number of people who see the original headline on Yahoo or who click on it.

Again, the virality—the clickiness and stickiness—of the original headline is critical. First, it has to catch the eye of the people at Yahoo who do the reposting. Then, that headline must be good enough to get a reasonable fraction of Yahoo readers to actually click, and then stick around long enough to click on the "Read More" link and come to ThinkProgress. It seems likely 20 to 50 times as many people see the original headline on Yahoo as ever get to ThinkProgress. I've had posts with tens of thousands of page views that came from Yahoo.

Additionally, the headline is crucial because people find online content when they are searching for a related topic. When you do a search, the most popular headlines from the most credible sites are generally shown first. You probably skim through the top posts, and click on the one that seems most relevant or most intriguing.

So the headline doesn't matter just because it determines how many people will actually read your post. It is literally the only part of your post the vast majority of people will ever see.

The headline test is a very rudimentary example of the power of big data—the ability to examine a large amount of information and process it in real-time to make better decisions than you would have otherwise made. But before I discuss big data's full power, and how Trump and the Russians used it to swing an election, let's look at ways to optimize your headlines if you don't have access to message testing.

IF YOU CAN'T DO MESSAGE TESTING, YOU MUST USE TESTED MESSAGES

If you are able to do online message testing, you still need to know the best headlines to test. If you can't do real-time message testing, then you at least want to use the most tested messages, the ones that have literally stood the test of time—and that modern social science and online analytics confirm are the best. In 2012, researchers Jonah Berger and Katherine Milkman published "What Makes Online Content Viral," a study of almost 7000 the *New York Times* articles to understand which ones make the newspaper's "most e-mailed list." They found that "content that evokes high-arousal positive (awe) or negative (anger or anxiety) emotions is more viral," but "content that evokes low-arousal, or deactivating, emotions (e.g. sadness) is less viral."

Recall the Grand Unified Theory (GUT) of going viral: Triggering the right emotions is most consistently achieved by telling a story using the figures of speech. The figures are the word patterns that survived thousands of years of storytelling, to the point where our brains became hardwired to respond to them.

No surprise then, that modern marketing studies have shown that the use of certain figures "leads to more liking for the ad, a more positive brand attitude, and better recall of ad headlines," as a 1992 article, "On Resonance: A Critical Pluralistic Inquiry into Advertising Rhetoric" explained. A 1994 analysis of more than two thousand print ads—"The Use of Figures of Speech in Print Ad Headlines" by marketing professor James Leigh—found that three-fourths of ad headlines use figures of speech, with the most common being puns ("Nothing runs like a Deere") and figures of repetition, such as alliteration ("Intel Inside"). Leigh notes that an earlier study of award-winning headlines "had a panel of creative directors categorize the headlines according to their commonalities and differences." Of the seven categories derived by their judges, he points out that "only one of them (news/information) does not have its basis in figures of speech."

Since my online writing focuses on news and information, along with commentary, many of my top headlines do not use figures—but a disproportionately large number do. ClimateProgress has always tweeted out the headlines, and even before we did headline testing, our headlines were typically retweeted as much as or more than blogs or websites with ten to fifty times the traffic. A key reason was the use of the figures of speech.

I analyzed headlines from 2011, a year ClimateProgress started off with only 10,000 Twitter followers (compared to 200,000 seven years later). I looked at the ones that were retweeted 250 to 1,000 times, which means they were potentially seen by 100,000 to 400,000 people. A high fraction of those viral headlines used one or more figures:

- Mother Nature Is Just Getting Warmed Up: June 2011 Heat Records Crushing Cold Records by 13 to 1 [*pun, personification*]
- 'Job-Killing' EPA Regulations for Chesapeake Bay Will Create 35 Times as Many Jobs as Keystone XL Pipeline [*irony*]
- Shale Shocked: "Highly Probable" Fracking Caused U.K. Earthquakes, and It's Linked to Oklahoma Temblors [*alliteration, pun*]
- Breaking News! Energy Efficiency Programs Are Working, Saving Consumers Millions [*sarcasm*]
- It's Not the Heat, It's the Stupidity: Limbaugh Calls Heat Index a Liberal Government Conspiracy [*pun*]
- Exxon Makes Billion-Dollar Bet Climate Change Is Real, Here Now and Going to Get Worse, But Keeps Funding Deniers [*irony*]
- NASA: It Rained So Hard the Oceans Fell [*metaphor*]

The key is not to have a purely figurative headline. A pun or clever turn of phrase that does not provide the essence of the article misses a crucial opportunity to inform the people who read only the headline.

In a webinar for *Forbes* online, the headline writer gave the following example of an improved headline. The original was "Abbott Ditches Its Drug Business." She changed it to "Amputation May Improve Abbott's Prognosis." The result of this personification and metaphor: In the hour before the change, the headline was clicked 795 times; in the one hour after the headline rewrite, that more than tripled to 2995.

The most liked tweet of all time came from former President Obama after a massive rally of neo-Nazis and white supremacists in Charlottesville, Virginia in August 2017 led to violent clashes that left three dead. In a series of three connected tweets, Obama wrote:

> No one is born hating another person because of the color of his skin or his background or his religion...
>
> People must learn to hate, and if they can learn to hate, they can be taught to love...
>
> ...For love comes more naturally to the human heart than its opposite – Nelson Mandela

The first tweet had 4.6 million likes and the next two had a combined 3 million likes. This quote, like most famous quotes, is filled with the figures, especially repetition and antithesis.

The winner of Twitter's first-ever Golden Tweet Award for the most retweeted tweet of 2010 was humorist Stephen Colbert for his BP disaster bon mot, "In honor of oil-soaked birds, 'tweets' are now 'gurgles.'" That combines a pun, sarcasm, and (one form of) personification. Chiasmus, pithy and profound, makes for a memorable tweet. The second most retweeted tweet of 2010 was from the rapper Drake: "We always ignore the ones who adore us, and adore the ones who ignore us." Not an original thought, but original thoughts are rare. The trick to going viral is to say an old truth in a new, pithy way.

Chiasmus also makes for a viral headline. *Forbes* posts the web statistics for its articles. One of its most widely read and shared posts of 2012 was a February piece on the debate over legislation on internet piracy headlined, "You Will Never Kill Piracy, and Piracy Will Never Kill You." The article has been viewed over 670,000 times, and the headline was likely viewed by millions.

BIG DATA AND THE TRUMP CAMPAIGN

Headline testing and analysis are one of the simplest uses of big data, which involves analyzing vast amounts of information rapidly to find patterns that improve decision making. But big data combined with artificial intelligence and machine learning can be far more powerful. Hence, this combination is rapidly driving more and more decisions in the political and corporate world. I've been able to see this power first-hand as an advisor to New Frontier Data, the leading big data firm providing actionable analysis in the cannabis sector.

I asked Gary Allen, New Frontier Data's Chief Operating Officer, for an example. Allen is a pioneer in data analytics who created the first mobile banking app in 1998 and then worked on market-leading search technology with companies like DoubleClick. Allen said the New Frontier data engine can "ingest the entire data stream of Instagram on a daily basis," even though Instagram surpassed 500 million daily active users in 2017. We can then apply machine learning and advanced search algorithms that "enable the correlation, collection, and understanding of all topics related to cannabis through the noise of all that data." The technology "captures photographs, messaging, interactions and responses, sharing, commenting, all again with the focus on cannabis itself."

So using big data, companies with emerging brands or multiple products can see the story of their product marketing unfolding as it's literally being written by their customers. Companies can see which products are trending up or down, for instance, or which demographics like the product most—and so should be targeted for more ads. We're seeing the emergence of so-called "results-driven cannabis products"—those that combine different strains and potencies to achieve a result such as "this product gives you energy," or "this product helps you sleep." Big data allows the makers of such products to get instant feedback on their customers' responses.

Every major company in the world is using data analytics to create and target their products. Imagine the value of such data ingestion and analysis in the fashion industry to designers and manufacturers trying to stay ahead of the latest fashion trends.

Now imagine someone had access to the entire datastream of Facebook—every post, comment, like and share you and your friends and two billion other people have made—so they could create detailed personality profiles of tens of millions of voters in this country and around the world. Imagine they could use those profiles and big data analytics to test messages and advertising on different micro-targeted groups of almost unlimited specificity *every day*—veterans in western Florida between the ages of fifty-five and sixty-five or occasional African-American voters in Philadelphia between thirty and fifty or Bernie Sanders voters in Wisconsin under thirty-five. Imagine they could test every aspect of an advertisement—not just the headline but the text itself, the image that goes with it, even the color or shape of the button people have to click to donate money to your campaign.

Facebook allows any advertiser, indeed, anyone with enough dollars—or rubles—this degree of analysis. Trump's presidential campaign tested an average of 50,000 to 60,000 micro-targeted ads a *day* on Facebook. Some days they tested more than 100,000, as Brad Parscale, the campaign's digital director explained on *60 Minutes* in 2017. That is serious message testing, and it allowed the campaign to raise a quarter-billion dollars on Facebook, while at the same time perfecting the clickiest and stickiest messages for every conceivable voter group, thereby swinging countless votes in key swing states.

Facebook has a huge number of tools to make this as easy as possible. For instance, suppose you know the names, email addresses, or phone numbers of your supporters, but not their Facebook page. No worries, that's what "Custom Audiences" is for. The company explains, "Just upload a list of contact info like email addresses or phone numbers," and "We'll deliver your ad to those people if they're on Facebook." But suppose, after you have a Custom Audience list of thousands of supporters, you'd like to find millions of more people just like them on Facebook? "Lookalike Audiences" does this. Facebook explains that once you have a "Custom Audience created with a data partner"—or with your mobile app data or fans of your Facebook Page—"we identify the common qualities of the people in it," using demographic or other information. "Then we find people who are similar to (or 'look like') them. Just like magic, you've got a vast number of new potential supporters you can target with custom ads. Finally, suppose you want to know the effectiveness of your marketing campaign? Just use "Brand Lift studies." The company explains, "Through the use of polling, a Facebook brand lift study can help advertisers understand how well their brand campaign resonated with people."

Parscale used all of those and more—with the help of Facebook itself. As he told *60 Minutes'* Lesley Stahl, the

Trump campaign had staff from Facebook (and Google and Twitter) embedded in its offices: "Facebook employees would show up for work every day in our offices." They were "helping teach us how to use their platform." He explained:

> I asked each one of them by email, "I wanna know every, single secret button, click, technology you have. I wanna know everything you would tell Hillary's campaign plus some. And I want your people here to teach me how to use it."

But "Facebook, Twitter, and Google [went] beyond promoting their services and facilitating digital advertising buys," according to a 2018 paper in the journal *Political Communication*. Based on interviews with campaign officials and workers from the social media giants embedded inside those campaigns, the analysis, led by journalism professor Daniel Kreiss, concluded that embeds were "actively shaping campaign communication through their close collaboration with political staffers."

A *Politico* story on the study noted that "Hillary Clinton's campaign declined to embed the companies' employees in her operations." Instead it decided to "develop its own digital apparatus and call in the tech firms to help execute elements of its strategy."

Parscale had even more help—from a big data company, Cambridge Analytica, which built a vast database of more than ten million persuadable voters to target using its analysis of their demographic information and psychological profiles developed from Facebook and other data. Cambridge Analytica helped the Trump campaign win by a narrow margin in key swing states by psychologically profiling millions of voters using data from Facebook, so those voters could be micro-targeted with messages tailored and tested to persuade them. The data was also used to advise the campaign on where Trump should visit based on where the biggest group of persuadable, undecided voters were. Also, by tracking the response to the micro-targeting in real-time on social media, the firm could provide guidance on which messages would resonate most with voters in the region being visited. The firm even tested a variety of political phrases and gave the campaign one of its most powerful metaphors, hashtags, and slogans "Drain the Swamp."

Breitbart executive board chair Steve Bannon, who became CEO of the Trump campaign in mid-August 2016, told *Bloomberg* in late October of that year, "I wouldn't have come aboard, even for Trump, if I hadn't known they were building this massive Facebook and data engine. Facebook is what propelled Breitbart to a massive audience. We know its power."

But in a bombshell statement released on March 17, 2018, Facebook admitted that much of the data Cambridge Analytica got from the social media giant on U.S. voters was obtained fraudulently. The firm "harvested private information from the Facebook profiles of more than 50 million users without their permission," according to a major *New York Times* investigation, "making it one of the largest data leaks in the social network's history." Later, Facebook admitted the number of hacked profiles was at least 78 million.

The firm—which had Bannon on its board and was backed by the same billionaire GOP donor, Robert Mercer, who backed Trump—was already under investigation by special counsel Robert Mueller for possible connections to Russian interference in the election. But in March, Facebook VP and deputy general counsel Paul Grewal accused the firm of running "a scam and a fraud," as he told the *Times*. The bottom line is chilling: The data theft, notes the *Times*, "allowed the company to exploit the private social media activity of a huge swath of the American electorate," for the purposes of electing Trump, who paid the firm millions of dollars in the closing months of the 2016 campaign.

They were worth the price, according to Carl Cameron, former chief political correspondent for Fox News Channel. Cameron, now Chief Communications Officer for New Frontier Data, told me that according to people he spoke to in the campaign at the time, Cambridge made the difference. The campaign knew Trump was behind in the key states of North Carolina, Pennsylvania, Wisconsin, and Michigan with over two months to go, but they were not able to budge the numbers despite all of Trump's efforts, including repeated visits to states like North Carolina. Too many voters simply didn't like Trump. But with the help of Cambridge Analytica's profiling, the campaign could identify a core group of voters who didn't much like either Trump or Clinton, particularly blue-collar voters, and micro-target them with tailor-made anti-Clinton messages aimed at swinging some toward Trump and depressing the vote of the rest. Cameron said the senior people in the campaign believe this final push made the difference.

Data-driven message testing matters.

CHAPTER NINE

James Cameron, 60 Minutes, Years of Living Dangerously: Revealing the Secrets Behind the Most Viral Videos

Visual storytelling of one kind or another has been around since cavemen were drawing on the walls.

– Frank Darabont, Director of *Shawshank Redemption*

... 90% of the videos in the sample contained elements of irony. Irony was the variable recorded most frequently in this study.

– "Going Viral: Factors That Lead Videos to Become Internet Phenomena," Elon University, 2011

[Our] research shows that, in order for climate science information to be fully absorbed by audiences, it must be actively communicated with appropriate language, metaphor, and analogy combined with narrative storytelling; made vivid through visual imagery....

—"The Psychology of Climate Change Communication," Columbia University, 2009

From August 2017 through January 2018, videos from the Years Project had a cumulative 200 million views on Facebook. And these are not cat videos or music videos or videos of Stormy Daniels or Stephen Colbert taking on

Donald Trump. These videos are on climate change and energy, which are not the sexiest or most innately viral subjects. But you don't need cats or Colbert to go viral—if you know the secrets behind viral video-making.

David Gelber, nine-time Emmy winner and co-creator of the Years Project, likes to tell the story of how he discovered many of these secrets during his quarter-century as a senior producer at *60 Minutes*, the most successful news magazine ever, and arguably the most successful TV show ever. After all, it "finished on the Nielsen Top 10 highest-rated programs list for 23 consecutive seasons," as CBS notes, "a feat that will probably never be equaled." Indeed, *60 Minutes* was the top show in America five different years, and the only show ever to achieve that in three separate decades.

So what were *60 Minutes'* secrets? Gelber relates one key lesson he learned from the show's creator and Executive Producer, Don Hewitt:

> I was early in my tenure at *60 Minutes* and I was very disposed to doing environmental stories, and I went to Don and I said to Don, "we need to do a story on acid rain" and he said, "Gelber, we don't do stories here about acid rain, we do stories about people who do something about acid rain." I thought that was a great lesson.

Without a good character to build a story around, Gelber explained there was no chance a segment would air: "You would drop the story or you would keep looking until you found someone." What made someone a good character? It was "somebody who could talk in a way that people would stop what they're doing on a Sunday evening and listen. I think we've replicated that in the two seasons of *Years* that we've done."

Gelber added, "We had a lot of training at *60 Minutes* in how to do stories that a large audience would want to watch." Here's another trick he learned:

> Every time I do a story—and maybe this is a lesson from Don—I try to project six months ahead and say, "What is it about this story that people are going to remember?" And if I didn't have that, I knew it wasn't that great a story. Television goes bad very quickly. It's very easy to forget what you've seen two or three days later. That's the nature of mass media these days.

For people to remember a story "It has to have emotion in it," Gelber explained. "If it's just information, it's not going to cut it. It could be very important and valuable information, but it's not going to last unless there's some emotional hook to it."

People are drawn to memorable stories about emotionally compelling people, as they have been for thousands of years. This may be the oldest technique there is, as we've seen, but like so many world-changing ideas, execution is hard.

I've been very fortunate to work with the viral video masters at the Years team from the inception, including the director James Cameron, one of the most successful visual storytellers of our time. Cameron's movies have grossed more than $6 billion, and he still holds the distinction of having directed the two all-time highest grossing movies worldwide, *Titanic* and *Avatar*.

In August 2010, Cameron invited me to spend a couple days with him at an Aspen, Colorado renewable energy conference—after he read a book of my ClimateProgress posts (see Introduction). We spent a lot of time brainstorming ideas for a climate change TV series when he wasn't being surrounded by fans and trying to talk to every last one of them. Cameron is simply the most creative person I've ever met. He came up with gem after gem but the idea that appealed the most was a docuseries focused on the stories of people at the front line of climate change, extreme weather, and clean energy solutions.

"This is one-hundred percent a people story," Cameron told me. Of course, that's been a core element of his success all along. Even when he used astonishing special effects to recreate one of the most famous disasters in history, the sinking of the *Titanic*, he infused it with an unforgettable love story about people we came to care about, Jack and Rose, played by Leonardo DiCaprio and Kate Winslet.

Coincidentally, several weeks after talking to Cameron, David Gelber and Joel Bach called me to explain that they were planning to leave *60 Minutes* to focus on climate documentaries. I had met them the previous year when they interviewed me for a climate story. Their idea was not that far from Cameron's, so I was confident he would be interested in working with them to achieve his vision. And indeed when Cameron did meet them, he quickly agreed to be an executive producer (EP). The late Jerry Weintraub— who produced such hits as the *Ocean's Eleven* remake plus its sequels—was already on board as an EP. And, with Cameron's help, Arnold Schwarzenegger, who had been a champion of climate action while California Governor, also joined as an EP and as a correspondent.

Even with all of this amazing talent, it still took over two years to find a home for the series, even though network executives kept telling us they loved the idea. Finally, Showtime signed us up, and the first season, nine one-hour episodes, aired in the spring of 2014.

The result is a master class in visual storytelling, one

you can watch on YouTube or the *Years of Living Dangerously* website. It won the Primetime Emmy for Outstanding Nonfiction Series that summer. *The UK Guardian* labeled it "the most important climate change multimedia communication endeavor in history." *Daily Kos* called it "the most important television series ever." An impact report on the series later found that "Of the 13 million [viewers] during the first six-month window of the show, *half of those people acted in some form*. Nearly a third shared information about climate change with others as a result of watching the show." The engagement with the show was so high that "one in six viewers voted in an election as a result of *Years*."

One reason the show was so engaging, so sticky, is that three out of four viewers came to realize that climate change "is relevant to their daily lives." But another key reason was the experience gained at *60 Minutes*—as well as further lessons learned from studying the science of effective climate change communications. Especially influential was a review and analysis on "The Psychology of Climate Change Communication," at Columbia University. It concluded that for climate information to be fully absorbed by viewers, the message needs to be presented with "narrative storytelling" and with "appropriate language, metaphor, and analogy," that is "delivered by trusted messengers" and "made vivid through visual imagery."

We had a second season on National Geographic Channel that was seen by even more people in this country and some 160 countries worldwide. But while the direct impact of the series was significant, the social media aspect of the effort began to have an even bigger impact. Indeed, by mid-2018, the show's Facebook page had 2.5 million followers and was adding 15,000 more each week. At the same time, Facebook had begun to boost its video promotion.

So The Years Project began focusing on creating short-form online videos, some two to five minutes long. The effort was remarkably successful, as noted early, with some 200 million total views in seven months. The average video had one million views, and the most watched, on Hurricane Irma, had 37 million.

Gelber credits co-creator Bach as the vital force behind these shorter viral videos, so I talked to the four-time Emmy winner about his secrets. Here are four:

1. "A good opening line of a video can make that video go viral."
2. "Tell your audience something they didn't know. But don't tell them what they should do. Let them see what's being done."
3. "What is essential for virality is a video that plays just as well with the sound on as with it off."
4. "Humor and irony are becoming vital story-telling components if you are going to get your word out on this issue and have a chance of going viral."

Bach explained that the opening line of a video is as important as the headline in a print article or online post. His philosophy goes further: You have to grab viewers for the first five seconds, and then grab them for the next five seconds, and the next five and the next—you need to assume you could lose viewers' attention at any instant because online, people are constantly inundated with an open fire hydrant of streaming choices.

Then Bach told me a startling statistic. Of the 37 million

people who watched the Hurricane Irma video, 26 million (70%) did so with the *sound off!* And for some videos, 90% of the views are with the sound off. So bold, easily read text is crucial. If your video doesn't work with the sound off, it doesn't work.

As for humor and irony, Bach noted that much of Season 2 was built around comedians as correspondents: David Letterman, Aasif Mandvi, Cecily Strong, and Jack Black. When it came to shorter videos, he pointed to a web series The Years Project did with the site Funny or Die, which starred then-Senator Al Franken in July 2017—before a series of accusations of sexual misconduct that fall led him to resign from Congress. The series was titled "Boiling the Frog," and most of the episodes co-starred Letterman, the king of irony. Subjects included why Letterman's beard is a weapon in the fight to control carbon emissions, and Letterman answering Franken's question, "Dave, when you were in India, why did you seem so stupid?" The series had more than 10 million views. You can find them at FunnyOrDie.com.

Interestingly, my most viewed post of all time, from June 2017, was headlined, "Rick Perry loses his cool when confronted by Sen. Franken on climate science." That post, which garnered half a million views, was built around a video of Franken's questioning of Perry that left the Energy Secretary sputtering. Later, I realized a key reason this video worked: Franken had constructed a compelling narrative (with the classic and-but-therefore framework). First, he noted that during Perry's confirmation, Perry said the climate was changing. But then, just the week before the hearing with Franken, Perry went on CNBC and denied the overwhelming scientific consensus that carbon dioxide is the primary driver of climate change. Therefore, the natural question was: "So if the climate is changing and if you disagree that CO2 is the primary driver, what do you think is driving the change?"

Perry stepped into the trap by repeating his anti-scientific claim. And when Franken explained that scientists have concluded "humans are entirely the cause" of recent warming—including, ironically, scientists funded by the conservative Koch brothers—Perry, one of the Trump's many cabinet-level climate science deniers, lost his composure and responded, "I don't believe it" and "I don't buy it."

THE MOST VIRAL VIDEOS ALL FIT THE SAME PATTERN

To repeat the Grand Unified Theory (GUT) of going viral: From the dawn of language through today, the most viral messages have always been stories told with the figures of speech that trigger key emotions and stick in the memory, such as metaphor, irony, and repetition.

Even today, the most viral videos are stories told with the figures of speech that trigger key emotions and stick in the memory. And like the most enduring of the ancient stories, these stories are set to music by a great bard, a term that derives from the ancient Celtic for minstrel-poet. These hip-hop and pop songs comprise 95 of the top 100 YouTube videos of all time, and no other class of videos comes close. Indeed two of the remaining five are music videos also—children's educational videos set to song and music, like "Wheels on the Bus." (The other videos are a toy review and two Russian children's cartoons.)

By March 2018, if you wanted to crack the top 100 YouTube videos of all time, you needed more than one billion views. Here are the top 25 listed along with their main artist and billions of views.

1. "Despacito" Luis Fonsi 5.1
2. "See You Again" Wiz Khalifa 3.5
3. "Shape of You" Ed Sheeran 3.4
4. "Gangnam Style" Psy 3.1
5. "Uptown Funk" 3.0
6. "Masha and the Bear: Recipe for Disaster" 2.9
7. "Sorry" Justin Bieber 2.9
8. "Sugar" Maroon 5 2.5
9. "Shake It Off" Taylor Swift 2.5
10. "Bailando" Enrique Iglesias 2.5
11. "Roar" Katy Perry 2.45
12. "Lean On" Major Lazer and DJ Snake 2.3
13. "Blank Space" Taylor Swift 2.30
14. "Hello" Adele 2.3
15. "Dark Horse" Katy Perry 2.3
16. "Thinking Out Loud" Ed Sheeran 2.2
17. "All About That Bass" Meghan Trainor 2.2
18. "Counting Stars" OneRepublic 2.16
19. "Chantaje" Shakira 2.1
20. "Wheels on the Bus" LittleBabyBum 2.1
21. "Closer" The Chainsmokers 2.1
22. "This Is What You Came For" Calvin Harris 2.0
23. "What Do You Mean?" Justin Bieber 1.9
24. "Baby" Justin Bieber 1.8
25. "Chandelier" Sia 1.5

Yes, these videos generally have superstars singing songs by top lyricists with world-class musicians, dancers, directors, and the like. But the point of this book is that these videos go viral because—at their core—they are all stories told with the figures of speech.

Consider "Despacito" ("Slowly"), which has surpassed an astounding five billion views. It's a classic story told figuratively: Boy meets girl, boy wants to have sex with girl, boy describes what the sex would be like. Of course, you don't need a translator to see and hear the song's rhyme and repetition. Those are core elements of pop songs globally. But here's a translation of one of the less X-rated verses:

> Slowly
> I want to undress you with kisses slowly.
> Sign the walls of your labyrinth
> and turn your body into a manuscript.

That's quite an extended metaphor.

Most of the top 100 are stuffed with metaphors or extended metaphors, which are often amplified by visual metaphors. In the video for Katy Perry's "Roar," Perry crawls through the jungle like a lion. Her smash, "Dark Horse," is another animal-themed, figure-filled song, with a video that is entirely an extended visual metaphor in which Perry is like a magical Cleopatra.

In 2010, Lady Gaga became the first musician in history to reach one billion online views with the help of two extended metaphors. The top-selling song of 2009 was Gaga's "Poker Face," an extended metaphor of love as a game of poker and chance. Another monster hit, "Bad Romance," is also an extended metaphor—love as a bad romance novel or film. In 2011, Gaga explained her songwriting philosophy on MTV.com: "I just like really aggressive metaphors—harder, thicker, darker and my fans do as well." Gaga carries that philosophy into her brand, where, as the online Gagapedia explains, she calls her fans "Little Monsters," a term they eagerly embrace online and in concerts. Her brand became inclusiveness—accepting people no matter how different they are, which was epitomized by her hit song, "Born This Way." I attended a 2017 Gaga concert with my daughter, and her fans come dressed in every conceivable costume, and scream with glee when she calls them her Little Monsters.

Taylor Swift and the expert song writers she works with understand that metaphors are at the heart of most successful pop songs. All three of Swift's songs on the list of top 100 YouTube videos have a metaphorical title. The phrase "Shake it Off" is a metaphor for recovering from a setback. In the video, Swift takes the idiom literally and turns her own awkward dancing into a visual metaphor for how she shakes off all the attacks on her. "Blank Space" is about the metaphorical list Taylor has of ex-lovers who supposedly think she's "insane," but she has a "blank space" on that list, to which she wants to add the guy in the video.

The third song, "Bad Blood," is another metaphorical idiom, meaning hostility or negative emotions between Taylor and someone who betrays her. Here, "blood" is the metaphor for emotions. The video is the story of a team of high-tech superheroes, many of them Swift's real-life celebrity friends, who find and fight the person who betrayed her and her team. The song is apparently an allusion to Swift's public feud with Katy Perry, making it a true metametaphor.

One of the quintessential qualities these viral videos share with the epic poems of the great bards is that they stick in the memory. Equally important, they feed our own addiction to repetition, one that we never outgrow from early childhood—the desire to re-listen to or re-watch or retell or re-sing a favorite song or story. Haven't we all listened to a new record, CD, or digital music file over and over again, as my daughter and I did with *Hamilton*? Haven't we all had a jingle play over and over and over in our heads even when we don't think we want to hear it? It's so common we've even created a metaphor to describe it—an earworm.

"When you plant a fertile meme in my mind you literally parasitize my brain," to repeat the quote from Richard Dawkins, "turning it into a vehicle for the meme's propagation in just the way that a virus may parasitize the genetic mechanism of a host cell." In his 1998 book, *Unweaving the Rainbow*, Dawkins discusses earworms as examples of these memes. He notes that they have been around a long time, citing Mark Twain's 1876 short story, "A Literary Nightmare," about Twain's "mind being taken over by a ridiculous fragment of a diversified instruction to a bus conductor with the ticket machine." The too-sticky refrain was "Punch, brothers! Punch with care! Punch in the presence of the passenjare!" and the rest of the jingle is a viral collection of rhyme, repetition, alliteration, assonance, and consonance.

Dawkins goes on to say:

> Memes can be good ideas, good tunes, good poems, as well as driveling mantras. Anything that spreads by imitation, as genes spread by bodily reproduction or by viral infection, is a meme. The chief interest of them is that there is at least the theoretical possibility of a true Darwinian selection of memes, to parallel the familiar selection of genes. Those memes that spread do so because they are good at spreading.

Dawkins notes that the "idea that some memes may be more infective than others because of their inherent properties is reasonable enough." But he doesn't do a deep dive into what those "inherent properties" may be, and so I'm trying to fill that gap here.

One of the reasons certain songs become memes that stick in our heads is their use of the figures of speech, which, as I've discussed, were the memorable language patterns that survived the Darwinian fight for survival over many thousands of years of repeated storytelling—rewiring our brains along the way to think in narrative terms and process information with metaphors and other figures.

CHAPTER TEN

Amazon, Branding, and Personal Character: How to Have a Viral Impact in Your Professional Life

Character may almost be called the most effective means of persuasion.

—Aristotle, *Rhetoric*

The most powerful person in the world is the story teller. The storyteller sets the vision, values, and agenda of an entire generation that is to come.

– Steve Jobs, 1994

Joining CreateSpace, Kindle Singles, and Kindle Direct Publishing, [are] eight new Amazon Publishing imprints.... Many [authors] write and tell us how we have helped them send their children to college, pay off medical bills, or purchase a home.

– *Jeff Bezos,* Annual letter to Amazon shareholders, 2013

When I tell people I'm self-publishing this book on Amazon, they tend to be surprised. But when I tell them I make seventy cents out of every dollar on all Kindle sales—triple or quadruple what most major publishers pay—they tend to be much more surprised, and they want to know how they can get in on the action. The fact is, anyone can.

Books are one of the classic ways to go viral in life. Think of all the famous people you remember—or that the world remembers—primarily or exclusively because of one or more books they wrote. But the publishing world is a classic old-media gatekeeper, deciding who gets a shot at passing through their pearly gates to potential fame and immortality. The expense of mass producing an initial run of books and distributing them around the country was, for a long time, simply too high a barrier to entry for competition.

But as Amazon founder Jeff Bezos explained to shareholders in his 2011 annual letter, "even well-meaning gatekeepers slow innovation." In fact, the reason I'm on Amazon is that after publishing seven books on climate change and clean energy and public policy, I was simply unable to get a traditional publisher to buy *Language Intelligence* several years ago. Yet it was easily my best-written book at the time—and my most marketable, I thought. I even had a jacket quote from the amazing progressive champion Van Jones (who now has his own show on CNN): "This book changed my life, and it can change yours, too. Joe Romm understands the secrets of persuasion and messaging and has distilled them into this must-read book."

I also had a very good agent help me improve the manuscript and craft the sales pitch. As a result, many leading editors and publishers saw it. But all of them rejected it over the course of 2011 and into 2012. Why? Well, one key answer is that while I had the traditional credentials to publish books on climate change and clean energy—and many publishers told me they would take a book from me on those subjects—my credentials as a successful communicator were all based on my website. And even though it had gone viral, that meant little to the traditional gatekeepers.

That's when a colleague told me about Amazon CreateSpace, which produces a print-on-demand paperback of your writing and distributes it online. Converting to a Kindle ebook is also easy. Back then, self-publishing was still dealing with the negative brand image of the old "vanity" presses, which charged you a lot of money to publish your book but had no real means of distribution. Amazon, however, had streamlined the entire process, put it online, made it vastly cheaper, and, most important, created a distribution platform second to none.

Language Intelligence became my best-selling book—some 12,000 copies to date and still selling dozens a month. And thanks to Amazon not taking 80 to 90 percent of the sales revenues the way traditional publishers do, this book generated the most direct income for me by far. I would have had to sell over 40,000 copies at a traditional publisher to make more money.

I say direct income because the biggest value of books for me and for the vast majority of non-fiction writers is almost always the indirect income that comes from the brand created by the book. In fact, my least successful book, my collection of blog posts, had the biggest indirect impact of them all since it turned out to be clicky and sticky with James Cameron.

Anyone who can do their own online marketing—and anyone can—should publish on Amazon. If you talk to authors you will find they have one consistent complaint: "The publisher didn't market my book." Yet most publishers don't appear to understand how to truly market a book in this new age of social media virality. So you're going to have to market your own book anyway if you want it to make money or have an impact. But if you're doing most of the work, shouldn't you keep most of the money?

The game-changing *Fifty Shades of Gray* series began

as fan fiction for the vampire-romance *Twilight* series on fan-fiction websites before it moved over to E.L. James' own website, FiftyShades.com. She then expanded it into a three-part series, with the first book released in 2011 by an Australian online publisher. When it got to Amazon UK, it started outselling the *Harry Potter* books. Now, 125 million books and three movies later, James and her books are a global brand.

But it started online. Yes, you probably won't replicate James' level of virality. But, if you've read her work, then you know her virality isn't about writing skill as traditionally defined. Indeed, in your niche, you're probably at least as good a writer as she is in hers. Online, you have so much more flexibility, so many more options to break through, than the all-or-nothing-at-all approach of selling a book to a traditional publisher. You could start with a $4.99 novella or $2.99 mini "how to" guide or initially publish for free to generate an audience.

A few years ago, I was an editor for my friend Nick Sparks' 125-page book on dating and communications, *As You Are: Ignite Your Charisma, Reclaim Your Confidence, Unleash Your Masculinity*. Sparks is a great dating coach, who has helped thousands of guys be their genuine selves when dating. He has a couple of YouTube videos online with hundreds of thousands of views. When he launched his book as a Kindle, he initially set the price at $0.99. With on online marketing push from his fellow coaches, it quickly became a #1 bestseller in the category of "Dating."

The "best possible marketing calling card," is how Sparks described the book to me. To go viral in life, as Sparks has, you need to first figure out your brand, your niche. As my life coach Adam Gilad likes to say, "The riches are in the niches."

IT'S A BRAND-YOU WORLD

We now live in a world where you need to find your own niche, tell your own story, and make your own brand. Nobody is going to do it for you. "It's a Brand-You World" as *Time* magazine put it in 2006. "Need a job? Or a love life? Personal-marketing consultants can help you stand out from the crowd." And the crowd is a lot bigger and noisier now.

In truth, "branding in one form or another has been around for centuries," as the 2007 article, "The Hot History and Cold Future of Brands," explained. The word derives from the Old Norse *brandr,* meaning "to burn," since that's how early farmers stamped their ownership on their livestock.

> A farmer with a particularly good reputation for the quality of his animals would find his brand much sought after, while the brands of farmers with a lesser reputation were to be avoided or treated with caution. Thus the utility of brands as a guide to choice was established, a role that has remained unchanged to the present day.

These days you also want your brand to be hot, but only metaphorically.

Significantly, there's an even more important word that has an almost identical etymology—*character*. The word derives from the mid-14th century, *carecter*, "symbol marked or branded on the body," which goes back to the Greek *kharakter*, meaning "engraved mark," also "symbol or imprint on the soul." Even in ancient Greece, *kharakter* also meant, by metaphorical extension, "a defining quality."

Your character is your most important personal brand. It's your defining set of qualities, and it's ultimately what someone is buying whenever you persuade them to enter into any type of relationship.

Why should an employer hire you rather than someone else? Why should they promote you over someone else? Why should anyone become your client or buy your product? Why should they invite you to speak? Why should someone go out on a date with you? Why should they go out on a second date with you? Why should someone become a follower of yours on Twitter or Facebook or Instagram or YouTube?

The core questions about your brand and character boil down to these: What is special about you or what you are selling? What problem are you going to solve for the person you are communicating with? And can you be relied on to deliver what you've promised?

But you have to do more than merely answer these questions. You have to persuade the listener to believe you, that you have a good character, one that will be consistent and reliable over time—that you are a man or woman "of your word." And that requires a memorable and emotionally compelling story, as we've seen, as well as a platform to communicate that story.

Amazon is but one of many such platforms. Twitter, Facebook, Instagram, your blog or website: these are all platforms that now allow you to bypass the traditional gatekeepers for telling your story—the news media, TV, radio, newspapers, and magazines. Indeed, Daria Musk, "the girl whose voice launched a thousand lines of code," used Google to bypass the gatekeepers of the music industry, as we will see.

Ultimately, every single interaction you have with someone, every conversation you have, every speech or public talk you give, everything you write online, is a chance to go viral. Equally important, every communication you have is a chance to build and amplify your brand and your character.

Your brand is your self-narrative, your story. Stories, as we've seen, are how we make sense of the world and our place in it. That's why most of the great stories, especially the hero's journey, are a voyage of self-discovery to learn what makes the hero special. Even superheroes need a brand. Are you like a spider? Or like a bat who becomes a caped crusader and a dark knight? Are you Gryffindor or Slytherin? All of the Disney princesses not only have their own signature story about why they are special, but they also have their own uniquely colored dress, which at one point I could actually identify, thanks to my daughter's love of all things Disney for many years.

Disney is one of the world's great brands, which you would expect from master storytellers. "Disney Parks and Resorts exist to make magical experiences come alive," explained one senior executive in a 2014 speech at a Hub Brand Experience Symposium. That's true of their movies, too.

Apple co-founder Steve Jobs understood the power of storytelling. His desire to match Disney's "monopoly on the storyteller business," as he put it, led him to acquire the Graphics Group from the Lucasfilm computer division for $5 million and re-launch it as a separate company, Pixar Animation Studios, in 1986—the year after he was fired from Apple Computer. Pixar's first full-length animated film, *Toy Story*, was released in 1995. Under Jobs, Pixar set the standard for animated storytelling, with hits like *Finding Nemo, Monsters, Inc, Up*, and the *Toy Story* sequels. Jobs sold Pixar to Disney in 2006 for $7.4 billion in stock.

Jobs returned to Apple in 1997 and became CEO. He then led the company, which had been near bankruptcy, on a journey to become the most valuable brand in the world with a series of game-changing and indeed, world-changing products, including iPod, iTunes, iTunes Store, Apple Store, iPhone, App Store, and the iPad. But equally important, Jobs brought his storytelling skills to sell those products and create incredible brand loyalty, starting with the "Think Different" ad campaign.

How did Jobs do that? In one of the most viral TED talks, "How Great Leaders Inspire Action," leadership expert Simon Sinek explains the secret. He says if Apple marketed products like everyone else, their pitch might be "We make great computers. They're beautifully designed, simple to use and user friendly. Want to buy one?" That, for Sinek, is "Meh." That is "how most marketing and sales are done, that's how we communicate interpersonally. We say what we do, we say how we're different or better and we expect some sort of a behavior, a purchase, a vote, something like that."

But Jobs did it differently. Apple's message, Sinek says, is "Everything we do, we believe in challenging the status quo. We believe in thinking differently. The way we challenge the status quo is by making our products beautifully designed, simple to use and user friendly. We just happen to make great computers. Want to buy one?" For Sinek, "*What it proves to us is that people don't buy what you do; people buy why you do it.*" Sinek's powerful and eloquent aphorism has become a mantra for many in the business world. I'd tweak it only slightly for individuals: "If you want people to buy whatever you're selling, you first need to get them to buy your story."

The cost of not having a brand story is high—you're a vessel without a chart or a map, without a home or a destination, moving in whatever direction the wind blows. You aren't reliable or dependable. And, when a storm inevitably hits, you don't have a reputation to act as a compass to keep you on course.

Consider Facebook. What is its "brand"? What is CEO Mark Zuckerberg's priority—people or profits? To the extent that Facebook has a widely known origin story, it's one written by someone else, Aaron Sorkin, for the movie *The Social Network*—and, fairly or not, it portrays a company founded on personal betrayal, on choosing profits over people.

To the extent that Facebook is known for a brand statement or slogan or motto or mantra, it's "Move Fast and Break Things." But what's kind of cute and cutting edge for a small but fast-rising and over-achieving underdog—what works for a David taking on Goliath—can backfire like a misused slingshot once you become the giant. Giants are often clumsy and break big things, like, say America's election process or the privacy of tens of millions of people. As *Wired* magazine explained in its March 2018 cover story, "Facebook's Two Years of Hell," that motto "wasn't just a piece of advice to his developers; it was a philosophy that served to resolve countless delicate trade-offs—many of them involving user privacy—in ways that best favored the platform's growth."

Facebook has two core branding problems. First, it is not in sync with its customers on a core value—privacy. Users want their data protected. In 2010, Zuckerberg said he believes privacy isn't a "social norm" anymore. Facebook's business model is built around selling your information to others and micro-targeting you through ads. Facebook has been more focused on serving its paying customers than on its users. As the saying in Silicon Valley goes, "If you're not paying for the product, you are the product."

Second, Zuckerberg has refused to accept that Facebook

has become the Goliath of the news media, even though this was a transformation he himself led. That has left it to others to tell the story of how "Back in 2012, the most exciting social network for distributing news online wasn't Facebook, it was Twitter," as *Wired* explained. But that wasn't acceptable to Zuckerberg, so he "pursued a strategy he has often deployed against competitors he cannot buy: He copied, then crushed." Facebook became "the dominant force in the news industry," but Zuckerberg never wanted the responsibilities or regulations that come with being a media giant, so he simply opened the floodgates to all news, real or fake, from journalists or Russian trolls.

So, when the news broke in March 2018 of how a data breach left Cambridge Analytica—and, through them, the Trump campaign—in possession of the personal data of tens of millions of American voters, which was used to micro-target and influence them, Zuckerberg had no story to tell and remained silent for several days. When Apple CEO Tim Cook was asked by MSNBC on March 28 what he would do if he was Mark Zuckerberg, he said: "I wouldn't be in this situation."

WRITE YOUR OWN STORY—OR OTHERS WILL

In politics and in life, much as in business, if you don't write your own story and tell it over and over again in many forms, you can be sure that those who don't like you will.

Trump is a master of such opposition branding. Jeb Bush didn't brand himself. Not only wasn't his choice of "Jeb!" a viable slogan about who he is or where he'd take the nation, but the only story it tells is of a guy running away from his last name—which is especially ironic since Jeb is an acronym for his actual name, John Ellis Bush. So if you think of anything when you hear the name Jeb Bush now, it's probably "low energy," the brand Trump gave him and repeated endlessly, amplified by the news media, which couldn't get enough of the razzle-dazzle of this one-man reality show.

Similarly, Clinton was not comfortable with branding and with the slogans, storytelling, and repetition it requires. When you think of her, it's hard to get Trump's label, "crooked Hillary," out of your head. Again, the media helped make that go viral because they kept airing Trump's smear—and kept reading it aloud when he tweeted it out. Most media outlets still print or read aloud whatever nonsense or smear he tweets out, which just further spreads and embeds it.

Opposition branding works against an opponent who doesn't know how to fight back. Try to remember the words President Obama used to explain why Americans needed healthcare reform in 2009 or any time after that. I doubt you can, but I'm pretty sure you can remember what the opponents of healthcare reform said about it:

- "government takeover of healthcare"
- "government rationing care"
- "No Washington politician or bureaucrat should stand between you and your doctor"

These weren't actually true of the healthcare bill that passed, but they were the poll-tested language GOP strategist Frank Luntz urged conservatives to repeat over and over again in a memo published online, "The Language of Healthcare 2009." He repeats the word "takeover" (Washington or government) a dozen times, and the words "rationing" and "bureaucrat" appear over two dozen times each in the memo.

Luntz practices what he preaches—and conservatives

preach what Luntz practices. And that kind of amplification makes branding work.

"The mistake of my first term—couple of years," Obama told CBS News in July 2012, "was thinking that this job was just about getting the policy right. And that's important. But the nature of this office is also to tell a story to the American people that gives them a sense of unity and purpose and optimism, especially during tough times."

Countries, communities, and families need repeated stories to create and sustain a group identity, just as much as individuals need them to create and sustain their personal identity, their brand, their character, especially during tough times.

THE GIRL WHOSE VOICE LAUNCHED A THOUSAND LINES OF CODE

For aspiring singer-songwriter Daria Musk, July 2011 saw one of the lowest points of her career followed within days by a digital rebirth. This is her story.

> Each fat raindrop that splashed off my guitar case seemed to fall in slow motion. They collected and puddled in the cracked sidewalk, slowly seeping into my sneakers and taunting the tears threatening to spill over the bottom edge of my eyelids. I was banging on the stage-door of a tiny dive bar in upstate New York, getting soaked. I'd only just arrived for the little set I was supposed to play that night and the whole incident already felt doomed. And it was, almost.

Musk had been raised by old-school musicians, and, as she told me in March 2018, "because I'd chosen heroes who were in bands who broke in the decades before I was born, I was doing this music thing the old-fashioned way, trying to wow random people who just happened to be within ear-shot when I played." That meant doing a lot of gigs. "It was Sisyphean to say the least," she explained. "People always seemed to love it when I sang, but getting to the people was harder than I thought it would be."

This night was the worst. Her amp short-circuited. The sound guy brought the wrong cables, and his mixer didn't match the configuration of her equipment. Her clothes were wet, she redefined bad hair day—"*And there were three people in the audience.*" But in that moment of near-despair, she noticed that one of the three was a guy who'd seen her play at a theater the weekend before. "He had actually followed me to this very wet level of Dante's Inferno to hear me sing again."

With that "tiny glimmer of hope in a hopeless-looking situation," Musk's mood changed. She had an epiphany:

> I was flooded with gratitude for being given another night when I could sing. So I belted with abandon and that little stage turned into Madison Square Garden. The bartender insisted, as I bundled up against the rain still coming down, that I was the real deal, he'd say he knew me when. That was the moment I remembered the call I'd gotten earlier in the evening.

That call, which her older brother made while she was standing outside the dive bar in the rain, was about a brand new social network—Google Plus (Google+). It had launched just a few days earlier. Musk learned the next day that Google+ had a built-in, ten-way video chat of the Google Hangout, designed for conference video-calls and the like. But Musk thought, "Maybe I could sing into this thing and play a show, without having to lug my guitars through the rain."

What would happen next was something no one at Google had envisioned. Three days later, she was standing in front of her laptop and its webcam, her studio equipment wired into its ports. She pressed the button to start the livestream and....

Silence. At first there was no one. But then a face popped in, and another, until every spot was filled. People from Norway, India, Portugal, Brazil, California and Texas. I saw the sunrise on a different continent through someone else's screen. When someone left, their spot instantly filled with someone new. I couldn't see it but a digital line around-the-block started forming.

The comment thread spread like wildfire: There was a girl singing in this video chat thing, and she'd been going for hours. I told them I'd keep going as long as they wanted to listen. This kind of audience, attention rapt, smiles wide, was what I'd always wanted.

That evening, she played for six-and-a-half hours in a show for hundreds of people around the world, who rotated in and out of the ten digital windows of Google+. She woke up the next morning to press coverage in different languages. But that was just the start.

A couple days later these new tech-savvy fans figured out how to stream the video feed so people could watch while they waited for one of those "front row" seats where I could see them. 9,000 people in 100 countries watched that one. The next was 200,000. It snowballed from there.

When I met Musk just a year later, she already had more than 1.5 million followers on Google+ and had spoken at TEDGlobal.

By spring 2018, almost six years later, she had more than 4 million followers, had given two more TED talks, and had been named one of the first "Future Now" artists for the Grammys. She tours the world regularly, from her room and "IRL" (in real life), as she says. But it started that week in July 2011, when she "broke live, online":

> And broke is the right word here. We crippled the system with the traffic and HD audio feeds and got a very confused call from Google when they went to fix it. I'm guessing it took at least a thousand lines of code to get it up to speed and build the new version I'd inspired with my singing (Hangouts On Air)
>
> I got welcomed into the tech community, as an accidental innovator and honorary geek. I started living the musical life I'd dreamed of by day and moonlighted as a consultant for some of the biggest tech and entertainment companies in the world.

She had discovered her purpose in the world, her origin story, and her brand—"the girl whose voice launched a thousand lines of code"—a millennial twist on a millennia-old story, one that launched the twin epic narratives of the greatest bard of yore, Homer. Musk had become, in her words, an "*artistpreneur*—someone who makes what they love, what they do—by bushwhacking a wonderfully unexpected path into my own future."

What advice does Musk offer those who also want to skip the whole "starving artist" cliché?

> Today we live in a world that's coo-coo for content. People need stories and books that help them cope with the crazy pace of being alive today. They need songs and movies that make them feel more connected to themselves and each other. Everyone needs someone

or something to make them feel seen and heard and less alone.

The minute I stopped waiting to be discovered, I discovered a whole world of people waiting with their arms wide open. People saw me, see them. I heard them, hear me. We connected in a deeply human way, from miles away. And when you feel real gratitude for each and every person you connect with online, see them as a friend and not a number in a social count or bottom line, it makes it all worthwhile. Then when you do go viral, you appreciate it more.

THE THREE STEPS TO WRITING YOUR OWN HERO'S JOURNEY

Musk learned the three key lessons of the hero's journey and of going viral in your professional life. First, you have to take that moment of adversity, that low point everyone hits, and rewrite the script so that it becomes your springboard to motivation and inspiration—part of your superhero origin story. Second, you have to understand what your superpower is, especially in the context of this new world of virality. What's your unique talent, the one that inspires passion and meaning? What problems can you help people solve? Third, every communication you make matters because it is a chance to make a connection, a chance to demonstrate your character and amplify your brand, a chance to help someone on their hero's journey.

Everyone has an origin story—a story of rebirth, sometimes called a "zero to hero" story—even Steve Jobs. As Jobs explained in his 2005 Stanford commencement address—a powerful story that went viral on YouTube—his zero point was being fired by Apple at the age of thirty. "Sometimes life hits you in the head with a brick," Jobs told the graduates.

"What had been the focus of my entire adult life was gone, and it was devastating. I really didn't know what to do for a few months," he explained. "I was a very public failure, and I even thought about running away from the valley. But something slowly began to dawn on me—I still loved what I did…. And so I decided to start over."

> I didn't see it then, but it turned out that getting fired from Apple was the best thing that could have ever happened to me. The heaviness of being successful was replaced by the lightness of being a beginner again, less sure about everything. It freed me to enter one of the most creative periods of my life.
>
> During the next five years, I started a company named NeXT, another company named Pixar, and fell in love with an amazing woman who would become my wife…. In a remarkable turn of events, Apple bought NeXT, I returned to Apple, and the technology we developed at NeXT is at the heart of Apple's current renaissance. And Laurene and I have a wonderful family together.

For me, like so many progressives, Trump's election was the brick to the head. Indeed, each week of his presidency, sometimes each day, feels like another brick. I'm fortunate to have work that allows me to respond to Trump. But I wanted to do more, especially after my brother Dave died. Hearing the stories of all the people he had touched spurred me to start working on this book intensively.

I also started working with an inspiring life and relationship coach, Adam Gilad, who happens to be an award-winning screenwriter and film producer. He encouraged me—and all of his students—to figure out our brand, to figure out how we could best leverage our skills and our passion to help people solve some serious problem in their personal or professional life.

Jobs explained to the Stanford grads that they need to figure out their passion in life because that's what saved him:

> I'm convinced that the only thing that kept me going was that I loved what I did. You've got to find what you love. And that is as true for your work as it is for your lovers. Your work is going to fill a large part of your life, and the only way to be truly satisfied is to do what you believe is great work. And the only way to do great work is to love what you do. If you haven't found it yet, keep looking. Don't settle. As with all matters of the heart, you'll know when you find it. And, like any great relationship, it just gets better and better as the years roll on. So keep looking until you find it. Don't settle.

Anyone looking for help honing in on their purpose and meaning in life would benefit from working with a coach like Gilad, as would anyone who has found what they love to do, but wants to become more focused and effective. My work with Gilad led to this brand statement:

> I help frustrated progressive change-makers master persuasive and memorable communications so that they become fearless viral superstars who have a huge impact on the world.

That brand statement also became a unifying theme for this book. Of course, you don't have to be a frustrated progressive to want to become a fearless viral superstar who has a huge impact on the world. But the world needs many more viral progressive superstars if we are going to resist Trump and preserve a livable climate. So that's my focus now.

Finally, one truth about virality is that every communication matters because we never know which one is going to go viral—and we never know which one will make a memorable and perhaps even life-changing impact.

Many years ago, I would sometimes debate climate change with conservatives on TV and radio or in person. My nemesis, the opponent I most feared, was Jerry Taylor of the libertarian Cato Institute, since he was both the craftiest and best communicator the other side had. So I was a bit worried when Taylor appeared at a small panel discussion on energy where I was presenting in 2016.

But to my surprise, during the discussion phase, he said, "I agree with what Romm said." We talked afterwards, and he explained he was now president of the Niskanen Center where he works to turn conservatives who deny climate science into climate activists. And he thanked me for helping inspire this metamorphosis. At the time, I thought Taylor was just being kind to a former foe, but then he began to tell his story publicly.

Here is Taylor's story as he related it in a 2017 interview with *The Intercept*, headlined "How a professional climate change denier discovered the lies and decided to fight for science." As he explained, back in the 1990s, "I was absolutely convinced of the case for skepticism with regard to climate science and of the excessive costs of doing much about it even if it were a problem. I used to write skeptic talking points for a living."

Sharon Lerner of *The Intercept* then asked him, "What was your turning point?" Taylor replied:

> It started in the early 2000s. I was one of the climate skeptics who do battle on TV and I was doing a show with Joe Romm. On air, I said that, back in 1988, when climate scientist James Hansen testified in front of the

Senate, he predicted we'd see a tremendous amount of warming. I argued it'd been more than a decade and we could now see by looking at the temperature record that he wasn't accurate.

After we got done with the program and were back in the green room, getting the makeup taken off, Joe said to me, "Did you even read that testimony you've just talked about?" And when I told him it had been a while, he said "I'm daring you to go back and double check this." He told me that some of Hansen's projections were spot on. So I went back to my office and I re-read Hanson's testimony. And Joe was correct. So then I talked to the climate skeptics who had made this argument to me, and it turns out they had done so with full knowledge they were being misleading.

I barely remember the conversation Taylor relates here, since I've had so many with conservatives over the years. But this particular one set Taylor on a path of rediscovery and rebirth. And that's the point: Every conversation you have is a chance to help someone on their hero's journey.

CHAPTER ELEVEN

Resisting Trumpism and Russian Cyberwarfare: Don't Bring a Knife to a Gun Fight

Social media facilitates the spread of a narrative outside a particular social cluster of true believers by commanding the trend.
—Lt Col Jarred Prier, "Commanding the Trend: Social Media as Information Warfare," Winter 2017

"We have three major voter suppression operations under way,"
says a senior [Trump campaign] official.... Trump's invocation
at the debate of Clinton's WikiLeaks e-mails ... was designed to
turn off Sanders supporters.
—"Inside the Trump Bunker, With Days to Go,"
Bloomberg, October 27, 2016

Trump confidant Roger Stone's success was having the connections
and creating the opportunities for Guccifer2.0 and other Russian
groups to really start taking advantage of social media and
pounding these negative memes that Hillary's a crook, et cetera.
—Carl Cameron, Former FoxNews chief political correspondent,
April 2018

The evidence keeps growing that the Russians coordinated their cyber-attack on the 2016 U.S. elections with the Trump campaign to support and amplify—to viral-ize—both pro-Trump and anti-Clinton messages. Russian intelligence and Putin's cyber-soldiers have mastered the dark side of virality. And they have used that mastery to launch an asymmetric attack on democracy in this country and around the world.

Russia's attacks continue today, as does the asymmetry, especially since President Trump continues to downplay the attacks or deny they ever occurred. But thanks to indictments of 13 Russians by special prosecutor Robert Mueller, along with information we've learned from our intelligence agencies and the media, we not only know of the staggering breadth of the Russian operation, we also know that senior members of the Trump campaign were knowingly in contact with Russian intelligence before the election.

In an extended series of interviews, former Fox News Channel chief political correspondent Carl Cameron helped me connect the dots between the Trump campaign, Russian intelligence, and the various Russian trolls around the world who were creating and viralizing memes and fake news on social media to help elect Trump. Cameron, who covered the Trump campaign in 2016 (and every other presidential election since 1988), also shed light on the key role big data firm Cambridge Analytica played, as I discussed in Chapter Nine.

Mastering the rules and secrets of virality is not merely something worth doing if you want to maximize your personal impact and reach millions with your messages and stories. It's a necessity if we are to ensure Lincoln's vision—"that government of the people, by the people, for the people, shall not perish from the Earth."

So, as the final example of how to go viral, *I will explore a few of the core strategies and tactics the Russians employed to help Trump sell his narrative and his memes*—and to thereby enable Trump's victory by "commanding the trend."

That's the apt term from U.S. cyberwarfare expert Lt. Col. Jarred Prier in a seminal 2017 article on "Social Media as Information Warfare." We are at war, even if our country's leader says we aren't.

HOW RUSSIA HELPED THE TRUMP CAMPAIGN WIN THE 2016 ELECTION

The Russians used every weapon imaginable to support Trump's campaign and amplify key pro-Trump and anti-Clinton messages. Russian cyber-warriors and their teams of troll mercenaries spread an astonishing amount of disinformation to boost Trump and hurt Clinton. Russian intelligence stole the emails of both the Democratic National Committee (DNC) and Clinton campaign chair John Podesta—and then leaked them with optimal timing to reinforce Trump's narratives and undermine Clinton's. And they paid a vast network of hackers and trolls to viralize Trump's memes and messages.

Disinformation has been a Russian specialty since the czars ruled, but Vladimir Putin took that expertise to the next level in 2016. Consider the repeated intervention in the campaign by then-FBI Director James Comey over the investigation into Clinton's use of a private email server as secretary of state—especially Comey's October's 28th letter to Congress asserting the FBI had "learned of the existence of emails that appear to be pertinent to the investigation." Famed data analyst Nate Silver headlined a detailed May 2017 analysis on his FiveThirtyEight website, "The Comey Letter Probably Cost Clinton the Election." He acknowledges Clinton made many costly mistakes on her own, but concludes the letter "halved Clinton's lead in the polls," and probably cost her the Electoral College since the election was so close in crucial swing states. Remember, late-deciding voters and those who couldn't decide which candidate they disliked the least swung strongly against Clinton (and no doubt many had been primed to do so from Clinton's "deplorables" comment).

Comey's decision appears to have been greatly influenced by Russian disinformation. As the *Washington Post* reported in May 2017, "a secret document that officials say played a key role in [Director] Comey's handling of the Hillary Clinton email investigation has long been viewed within the FBI as unreliable and possibly a fake, according to people familiar with its contents." In early March 2016, the FBI received "a Russian intelligence document claiming a tacit understanding between the Clinton campaign and the Justice Department" that the Department wouldn't "push too deeply" into the server investigation. The Russian document cited an alleged email that supported its claim. If true, it would have undermined the integrity of the FBI investigation. Thus, officials cited by the *Post* say it helped motivate Comey's public interventions and statements in the case.

"But according to the FBI's own assessment," the *Post* explained, "the document was bad intelligence—and according to people familiar with its contents, possibly even a fake sent to confuse the bureau." And although the FBI never found the underlying email the Russians cited, "senior officials at the bureau continued to rely on the document before and after the election" to help justify their handling of the case.

Here's another example of the power of Russian disinformation. A postelection analysis by BuzzFeed found that in the final months of the campaign, the "top fake election news stories generated more total engagement [8.7 million shares, reactions, and comments] on Facebook than top election stories from 19 major news outlets combined," which had 7.4 million. The overwhelming majority of the most viral stories from the real news outlets were skeptical or negative about Trump.

But the overwhelming majority of the most viral fake news stories were anti-Clinton or pro-Trump. Moreover, a large fraction of those came from sites like Ending the Fed, identified as a "Russian propaganda outlet," in a postelection analysis by an independent team of U.S. experts in computer science, statistics, and national security at the website PropOrNot. The rest came from websites that only publish hoaxes or are what BuzzFeed called "hyperpartisan websites."

Here are the top five fake news stories in the three months before the election with source and engagement in parentheses (and remember, the number of people who saw those headlines is vastly larger than the number who engaged with a story via a share, reaction or comment):

* Pope Francis shocks world, endorses Donald Trump for president (Ending the Fed, 960,000)
* WikiLeaks CONFIRMS Hillary sold weapons to ISIS … Then drops another BOMBSHELL (The Political Insider, 789,000)
* IT'S OVER: Hillary's ISIS Email Just Leaked & It's Worse Than Anyone Could Have Imagined (Ending the Fed, 754,000)
* Just read the law: Hillary is disqualified from holding any federal office (Ending the Fed, 754,000)
* FBI agent suspected in Hillary email leaks found dead in apartment murder-suicide (Denver Guardian, 567,000)

Now that's shock and awe. Or, rather, each of those headlines is aimed at stimulating at least one of the three high-arousal emotions that make content more viral—anger, anxiety, and awe. Unfortunately for those fighting fake news, as I do at ClimateProgress, lies have an obvious advantage over the truth: You can make up any headline and any story you want, and so it is much easier to create something clicky and sticky. That's one reason Donald Trump, the fossil fuel companies, and others pushing climate science denial over the years have been so successful.

"A compelling story, even if factually inaccurate, can be more emotionally compelling than a dry recitation of the truth," as GOP messaging strategist Frank Luntz advised conservatives in his infamous 2002 memo urging politicians to pretend to care about the climate while opposing serious action. Indeed, a March 2018 study, "The spread of true and false news online," by M.I.T. researchers in the journal *Science*, concluded:

> False news reached more people than the truth; the top 1% of false news cascades diffused to between 1000 and 100,000 people, whereas the truth rarely diffused to more than 1000 people. Falsehood also diffused faster than the truth. *The degree of novelty and the emotional reactions of recipients may be responsible for the differences observed.*

Sadly, falsehoods diffused significantly farther, faster, deeper, and more broadly than the truth in all categories of information, and the effects were more pronounced for political news.

But the Russians did much more to elect Trump than just promote novel and emotionally compelling disinformation. Russian military intelligence (the GRU) stole the Democratic National Committee (DNC) emails. The release of those emails helped create and support the narrative that the DNC favored Clinton over Sanders, which the Trump campaign and Russian trolls would use as a core part of their strategy to suppress the vote of disaffected Bernie Sanders voters in the general election.

That this narrative had some basis in truth made it more effective. But the Russians and WikiLeaks also misrepresented the emails. For instance, WikiLeaks made public various DNC emails from May 2016 days before the Democratic convention "that made it appear as if the DNC was solely pulling for Clinton," as *Newsweek* put it. But "in many online postings, the date was removed so readers would have no idea unless they searched for the original document that [it] was written at a time when Sanders could not possibly have won the nomination."

The GRU also hacked Clinton campaign chair John Podesta's emails. The Russians released those emails through WikiLeaks with perfect timing for Trump—one hour after Trump's infamous *Access Hollywood* tape from 2005 was made public a month before the 2016 election. Those emails became a key part of the narrative used to undermine the impact of Trump bragging that he often grabbed women "by the pussy." Indeed, the Russians and WikiLeaks kept dripping out these emails day after day, like a literal leak—and while there was nothing very scandalous in any individual email, they provided the kind of political gossip irresistible to mainstream media. Also, the constant coverage no doubt helped lead many voters to conflate those emails with the emails on Clinton's server, which Trump kept linking to his "crooked Hillary" meme.

But the Russians did much, much more. They had a massive troll army in our country and theirs engaged in disinformation. The Internet Research Agency (IRA) alone housed some 1,000 professional hackers and trolls in one St. Petersburg building in 2015, a mere two years after the agency's founding. They created a huge number of fake posts and fake comments, with a quota of 100 comments a day. One worker told the *Washington Post* in 2018:

> I immediately felt like a character in the book *1984* by George Orwell—a place where you have to write that white is black and black is white. Your first feeling, when you ended up there, was that you were in some kind of factory that turned lying, telling untruths, into an industrial assembly line.

Using the IRA and others, "Russia hijacked social media through propaganda narratives, true believers, cyber warriors, and a bot network," as Lt. Col. Prier explains. A crucial turning point occurred in September after Clinton's memorably misguided metaphor where she put half of Trump's supporters into a "basket of deplorables." Before that comment, Russian trolls "primarily used an algorithm to rapidly respond to a tweet from Donald Trump," but tweets and retweets about "deplorables" were so popular, notes Prier, that some trolls "became powerful voices with large followings; Trump himself frequently retweeted many of those users."

Indeed, many Russian trolls quickly put the word "Deplorable" in their name, since that "was all one needed to suddenly gain a network of followers numbering between 3,000 and 70,000." One troll who had tweeted under the alias of a black man and had 1,000 followers changed his name to "Deplorable Lucy"—and the profile picture "became a white, middle-aged female with a Trump logo at the bottom." Within days, he had 11,000 followers, and his core network of followers quickly embraced the "Deplorable" brand.

Prier explains the result:

In short, they were now completely in unison with a vast network of other Russian trolls, actual American citizens, and bot accounts from both countries on Twitter. With a large network consisting of Russian trolls, true believers, and bots, it suddenly became easier to get topics trending with a barrage of tweets. The Russian trolls could employ the previously used tactics of bot tweets and hashtag hijacking [taking a pro-Clinton hashtag and bombarding it with anti-Clinton smears], but now they had the capability to create trends.

Ultimately, the entire "Deplorable Network" was huge, Prier notes: "200,000 Twitter accounts consisting of Russian trolls, true believers, and bots." He estimates that, by itself, the network of bots—automated Twitter accounts that could rapidly send out huge numbers of tweets—consisted of between 16,000 and 34,000 accounts. Russia's most effective Twitter trends, he explains, came after the *Access Hollywood* tape was made public, where the network worked together "to drown out negative attention to Trump on Twitter." They did this by hyping Podesta's stolen emails, which Russian intelligence had stolen and which WikiLeaks began dribbling out starting just one hour after the tape was released. Prier concludes, "The cohesiveness of the group indicates how a coordinated effort can create a trend in a way that a less cohesive network could not accomplish."

But the depth and breadth of the Russian trolling operation wasn't clear until February 2018, when Mueller announced a federal grand jury indicted the IRA, two other groups, and 13 Russians with a broad conspiracy that "had as its object impairing, obstructing, and defeating the lawful governmental functions of the United States by dishonest means in order to enable the Defendants to interfere with U.S. political and electoral processes, including the 2016 U.S. presidential election." By 2016, the Russians "engaged in operations primarily intended to communicate derogatory information about Hillary Clinton, to denigrate other candidates such as Ted Cruz and Marco Rubio, and to support Bernie Sanders and then-candidate Donald Trump."

Anyone wanting to understand the cyberwar strategy and tactics the Russians use against this country and many others, and any American who is concerned about the future of our democracy, should read the whole indictment. Here are some highlights of both illegal and legal actions by the IRA:

> IRA employees, "were tasked to create social media accounts that appeared to be operated by U.S. persons" and ordered to create "political intensity through supporting radical groups, users dissatisfied with [the] social and economic situation and oppositional social movements."

> The IRA "used, possessed, and transferred, without lawful authority, the social security numbers and dates of birth of real U.S. persons without those persons' knowledge or consent" and posted on IRA-run social media accounts using these stolen identities.

> The IRA also "created and controlled" the "Tennessee GOP" account, which had the handle @TEN_GOP. "The @TEN_GOP account falsely claimed to be controlled by a U.S. state political party. Over time, the @TEN_GOP account attracted more than 100,000 online followers."

> "To measure the impact of their online social media operations, Defendants and their co-conspirators tracked the performance of content they posted over social media. They tracked the size of the online U.S. audiences reached through posts, different types of engagement

with the posts (such as likes, comments, and reposts), changes in audience size, and other metrics." The IRA routinely had experts review posts "to ensure they appeared authentic—as if operated by U.S. persons. Specialists received feedback and directions to improve the quality of their posts" including "guidance on: ratios of text, graphics, and video to use in posts; the number of accounts to operate; and the role of each account."

The viral impact of these activities was enormous. Consider an October 2017 article on The Daily Beast headlined, "Trump Campaign Staffers Pushed Russian Propaganda Days Before the Election." It points out that three weeks before the election, Trump's digital director Brad Parscale retweeted a @Ten_GOP post reading: "Thousands of deplorables chanting to the media: 'Tell The Truth!' RT if you are also done w/ biased Media!" Donald Trump Jr. followed the account and "retweeted the account three times, including an allegation of voter fraud in Florida one week before the election." Kellyanne Conway, then Trump's campaign manager, tweeted a post by the fake account. The tweet said, "Mother of jailed sailor: 'Hold Hillary to same standards as my son on Classified info' #hillaryemail #WeinerGate."

The Russian trolls did more than post on social media. As the campaign heated up, they became increasingly involved in political rallies. For instance, the indictment (which refers to the Internet Research Agency as the "ORGANIZATION") explains:

> In or around the latter half of 2016, Defendants and their co-conspirators, through their ORGANIZATION-controlled personas, began to encourage U.S. minority groups not to vote in the 2016 U.S. presidential election or to vote for a third-party U.S. presidential candidate.

Starting in approximately June 2016, Defendants and their co-conspirators organized and coordinated political rallies in the United States. To conceal the fact that they were based in Russia, Defendants and their co-conspirators promoted these rallies while pretending to be U.S. grassroots activists who were located in the United States but unable to meet or participate in person.

In order to build attendance for the rallies, Defendants and their co-conspirators promoted the events through public posts on their false U.S. persona social media accounts. In addition, Defendants and their co-conspirators contacted administrators of large social media groups focused on U.S. politics and requested that they advertise the rallies.

In or around late June 2016, Defendants and their co-conspirators used the Facebook group "United Muslims of America" to promote a rally called "Support Hillary. Save American Muslims" held on July 9, 2016 in the District of Columbia. Defendants and their co-conspirators recruited a real U.S. person to hold a sign depicting Clinton and a quote attributed to her stating "I think Sharia Law will be a powerful new direction of freedom."

On or about August 18, 2016, Defendants and their co-conspirators sent money via interstate wire to another real U.S. person recruited by the ORGANIZATION, using one of their false U.S. personas, to build a cage large enough to hold an actress depicting Clinton in a prison uniform.

These examples are but a sample of what's in the 37-page indictment. And the indictment is simply what Mueller had enough evidence to persuade the grand jury of. The full extent of the Russians' war on our democratic process and what Mueller knows remains to be seen. The indictment states "some Defendants, posing as U.S. persons and without revealing their Russian association, communicated with unwitting individuals associated with the Trump Campaign." But, as legal experts have pointed out, the indictment's repeated reference to "defendants and their co-conspirators" suggests that there are more people who will be charged, people who were not so unwitting.

HOW THE TRUMP CAMPAIGN AND THE RUSSIANS COORDINATED THEIR MESSAGE

As Carl Cameron explained to me, the goal of long-time Trump advisor and surrogate Roger Stone was to get Trump elected. Stone had encouraged Trump to run for years, and in 2000 he worked on Trump's brief run for the Reform Party presidential nomination. In 2016, he helped Guccifer2.0 and other Russian-backed groups boost an anti-Clinton narrative online targeted at key groups. Stone direct-messaged with Guccifer2.0 on Twitter—and emailed WikiLeaks editor Julian Assange—in August 2016. Stone denies this was collusion, but as Cameron explains, "it's important to know that Roger's entire career was based on doing dirty tricks. He boasted about it from the time he was in college until today."

Guccifer2.0, who claimed credit for giving WikiLeaks the DNC's stolen emails, had been masquerading as a self-described "lone hacker." Stone amplified that phony narrative in an August piece for Breitbart News, Steve Bannon's viral pro-Trump fake news site. In a piece headlined "Dear Hillary: DNC Hack Solved, So Now Stop Blaming Russia." Stone asserted: "I think I've got the real culprit. It doesn't seem to be the Russians that hacked the DNC, but instead a hacker who goes by the name of Guccifer2.0."

But, FBI investigators were able to track Guccifer2.0

online and determined he was an officer of Russian military intelligence, as The Daily Beast reported in 2018. Significantly, on August 4th, 2016 Stone sent an email to then-Trump adviser Sam Nunberg saying, "I dined with my new pal Julian Assange last nite." The email also suggested Assange had material that could help Trump overcome Clinton's big lead in the polls. On the same day, Stone appeared on hyperpartisan pro-Trump InfoWars radio show and explained Assange had "devastating" information about "Clinton Foundation scandals." Stone claimed that while the Clinton campaign argued there was no proof of those scandals, "I think Julian Assange has that proof and I think he is going to furnish it for the American people." Stone also said he spoke with Trump a day earlier, on August 3rd.

On August 10, Stone told a local Florida GOP group, "I've actually communicated with Julian Assange." CNN points out that on August 12, Stone said he knew Assange had some of Clinton's emails, "And I believe he will expose the American people to this information in the next 90 days." On August 14, Stone exchanged direct messages with Guccifer2.0. And on August 21, Stone tweeted, "It will soon be Podesta's time in the barrel," implying Stone had early inside knowledge that Podesta's emails had been stolen—which they had been, also by the GRU.

Indeed, as discussed above, those emails were made public by WikiLeaks two months later, with perfect timing for Trump—one hour after Trump's infamous *Access Hollywood* tape was made public on October 7. They became a key part of the narrative used to drown out the negative attention Trump's remarks were getting with a deluge of social media alternative story lines.

And no one did more to help WikiLeaks go viral than Trump himself—as ThinkProgress pointed out in a post headlined, "Trump mentioned WikiLeaks 164 times in last month of election, now claims it didn't impact one voter." Trump spoke about the WikiLeaks emails or their content over and over again from October 10 to election day in speeches, media appearances and debates. He said things like, "Boy, that WikiLeaks has done a job on her, hasn't it?" and "We love WikiLeaks. WikiLeaks." and "The media is an extension of the Clinton campaign as WikiLeaks has proven, and they will not talk about WikiLeaks."

Trump may not be good with the truth, but he has mastered repetition.

The cyber-bombshells kept dropping as I was writing this book. In late December 2017, we learned that George Papadopoulos, a Trump campaign foreign policy adviser, told an Australian diplomat in May 2016 that the Russians have a lot of dirt on Clinton in the form of thousands of emails stolen to embarrass her—and that he had learned about this weeks earlier directly from Russians associated with the Kremlin. This was months before Trump publicly asked for Russian help. "Russia, if you're listening, I hope you're able to find the 30,000 emails that are missing. I think you will probably be rewarded mightily by our press," Trump said on July 29. Hours later, he tweeted "If Russia or any other country or person has Hillary Clinton's 33,000 illegally deleted emails, perhaps they should share them with the FBI!"

Robert Mueller's team filed court documents on March 27, 2018 claiming that Trump campaign chair, Paul Manafort, and his deputy, Rick Gates, were communicating with someone ("Person A") who the FBI says "has ties to a Russian intelligence service and had such ties in 2016." The filing indicates one of Gates' associates stated "that Gates told him Person A was a former Russian intelligence officer with the GRU."

Recall that Manafort and Gates had both been indicted by a grand jury in 2017 and 2018 for multiple counts of bank fraud and conspiracy committed during their years working as "unregistered foreign agents" for the pro-Russian government of Ukraine. Gates pled guilty of two felonies—lying to investigators and conspiracy. A 2018 court filing by Mueller revealed that Deputy Attorney General Rod Rosenstein had written a memo in August 2017 authorizing Mueller to investigate Manafort for alleged "crime or crimes colluding with Russian government officials with respect to the Russian government's efforts to interfere with the 2016 election." In the filing, Mueller explains "the investigation covers ties that Manafort had to Russian-associated political operatives, Russian-backed politicians, and Russian oligarchs."

Coincidentally, Manafort was in the June 2016 Trump Tower meeting where Donald Trump Jr. and the president's son-in-law, Jared Kushner, met with a Russian lawyer connected to the Kremlin (and four other Russians) after being promised in an email "official documents and information that would incriminate Hillary and her dealings with Russia and would be very useful to your father." Trump Jr. responded to that email, "if it's what you say I love it especially later in the summer"—yet another example of message coordination.

Later, when the news of that meeting broke, the White House issued a statement claiming it was about adoption of Russian babies. We subsequently learned that Trump insisted on putting out this false statement—and Mueller is investigating whether that might be part of an obstruction of justice case against the President.

It would take an entirely separate book to explain all of the connections between Russia and Trump campaign officials that those officials initially lied about. But the point of my brief summary here is to underscore that to understand the thermonuclear impact the Russian cyber-attack had in helping elect Trump you must understand virality—and how the information revolution and rise of social media have changed the rules of going viral in recent years.

Progressives have brought a knife to a gun fight. "I hate to say it, but it seems like the creative instincts and the sophistication [of the Russians] exceeds a lot of the U.S. political operatives who do this for a living," CNN commentator Brian Fallon told the *Washington Post* after the IRA indictment was released. Fallon, who served as press secretary for Clinton's 2016 campaign, added, "There were memes and advertisements that were really in sync with the Trump campaign's rhetoric. The messages were in sync, and they certainly exploited some of our vulnerabilities."

HOW TO RESIST TRUMP, GO VIRAL, AND REACH MILLIONS

All those who want to resist Trump—and all those who care about preserving and protecting democracy from Trumpism and the Russians—will need to significantly up their game. To help defeat the dark side of virality, you'll need to master all of the skills laid out in this book. These skills are based around the five rules for consistently creating content that can go viral:

1. STORY: Tell a compelling story—but use the simple And-But-Therefore formula.
2. FIGURES OF SPEECH: Use the most unforgettable figures of speech, especially repetition, irony, and metaphor.
3. EMOTION: Trigger one of three activating

emotions that trigger content sharing.
4. MEMORABLE ELEMENTS: Select the most memorable words, phrases, and stories.
5. TESTING: Embrace message testing and tested messages.

These five strategies are really one overarching strategy, which is the Grand Unified Theory of going viral: To be as memorable and persuasive as possible, your message must trigger the right emotions, which is most consistently achieved by telling a simple, compelling story using the figures of speech. Those are the most tested viral messages in all of human history.

Today, big data and social media allow you to go a step further and learn the specific words and images that your audience finds most clicky and sticky—by testing multiple headlines and messages online. Whether you test or not, you should be spending much more time on writing the headlines for your posts, the subject lines of important emails, and the openings of all your public communications, whether they are videos or tweets or even speeches. After all, even a live audience can choose from countless alternatives on their cell phone once they conclude you're just one more speaker who can't or won't tell them an emotionally compelling story using the figures of speech.

Mastering these skills is not easy. Indeed, as the young Winston Churchill noted over a century ago in his metaphorically titled essay, "The Scaffolding of Rhetoric," the full set of secrets of persuasion are "known to very few":

> Of all the talents bestowed upon men, none is so precious as the gift of oratory. He who enjoys it wields a

power more durable than that of a great king.... The subtle art of combining the various elements that separately mean nothing and collectively mean so much in an harmonious proportion is known to very few.... The student of rhetoric may indulge the hope that Nature will finally yield to observation and perseverance, the key to the hearts of men.

Even after spending two decades studying these skills and working on my book *Language Intelligence*, a lot of my verbal communication was still blah, blah, blah as my daughter put it in 2010. One friend who read the book in 2012 told me, "You know, you don't talk that way."

I have to consciously practice these rules in order to overcome over a decade of being taught not to speak simply, not to repeat myself, not to tell stories. The higher education system, especially for scientists, is skeptical of storytelling if not outright anti-story. But then, a major goal of the Enlightenment especially the scientific revolution led by Newton was to replace a story-based explanation for the world with a reason-based explanation. The story about rainbows being a sign from God that he's not going to send us any more floods gets replaced by the basic science and math of reflection and refraction of light in water droplets.

But "no one ever made a decision because of a number. They need a story," explains Dan Kahneman, in Michael Lewis' 2017 book, *The Undoing Project*. Kahneman won the 2002 Nobel Prize in Economics for his pioneering work on the psychology of decision-making. In his best-seller *Thinking, Fast and Slow*, Kahneman notes, "The confidence that individuals have in their beliefs depends mostly on the quality of the story they can tell about what they see, even if they see little."

So mastering persuasion and virality requires that you, like me, overwrite or undo the bad brain reprogramming we received from years of misguided teaching on how to communicate with and persuade people. That's why I suggest memorizing Miranda's musical masterpiece *Hamilton*, since it is the quintessence of the five rules. And that's the final reason you should consciously treat every communication you make as a chance to go viral—because that's the best way to rewire your brain.

Epilogue and Epitaph: My Brother's Keeper

... their glory remains eternal in men's minds, always there on the right occasion to stir others to speech or to action. For famous men have the whole earth as their memorial.... in people's hearts their memory abides and grows.

—"Pericles' funeral oration," Thucydides, *History of the Peloponnesian War*

The telling and retelling of stories is the powerful means by which cultures of families and communities are formed and maintained, national identities are preserved ... and moral values are instilled. Stories can inspire, uplift, and transform their listeners, or they can belittle, humiliate, and drive their listeners to despair.

—Lewis Mehl-Madrona, M.D., *Coyote Wisdom: The Power of Story in Healing*, 2005

We must regain the conviction that we need one another, that we have a shared responsibility for others and the world, and that being good and decent are worth it.

—Pope Francis, *Encyclical Letter on Care for Our Common Home*, 2015

A long time ago my brothers and I met Mark Hamill—or at least Dave did. My mother bought us tickets to see a 1984 revival of Arthur Miller's classic play *Death of a Salesman* starring Dustin Hoffman and John Malkovich on

Broadway. I remember nothing about the performances except that I thought they were astonishing.

I do remember thinking that the person sitting in front of us looked very familiar. And I remember he was the first person on his feet applauding when the show ended. As we all stood up and applauded, I leaned over to Dave and whispered, "Isn't that Luke Skywalker?" When the applause died down, Dave said to him, "Are you—?" Hamill instantly interrupted, asking, "Why don't you give me some initials?" He clearly did not want his name blurted out in public. But someone did blurt it out, so he started walking toward the aisle.

I remember my brother instantly walking toward the aisle, too, so I followed him. He really wanted to say hello. Or, rather, when he did catch up, he wanted to tell Hamill that he had played the part of Luke Cakewalker in the Shockwave Radio Theater performance of the pun-filled "Food Wars" ("May the Fork be with you"). I think he handed Hamill one of his cards. I have no other memories of the event, although I do know that back then, in my early 20s, I wasn't the kind of extrovert Dave was, to pull that off, but then he was a fellow performer who played the same role as Hamill. Sort of. That was Dave.

That memory has replayed in my mind again and again—when I saw *The Last Jedi* with my daughter, when I write about Joseph Campbell or on the rare occasion when Hamill likes a ThinkProgress tweet of one of my articles. *The Last Jedi* is the final hero's journey for Luke. In his final deed, he dies heroically for a greater cause. Luke's mythic journeys have inspired millions.

My brother and his journey have been a life-changing inspiration to me, as I've related, especially the stories of how he touched so many different people and how he overcame his animosity toward my father. So I am one of the keepers (and sharers) of my brother's memories. But the point of these heroic stories and memories is "to stir others to speech or to action" as the great Athenian politician Pericles said in his famous eulogy for those killed in the first year of the Peloponnesian War. That speech was aimed at unifying wartime Athens with a shared story of preserving their unique culture, principles, and democracy—much as Lincoln used his speech remembering those who died at Gettysburg to help unite the Union in a common wartime purpose of preserving our democracy and our core principles that "all men are created equal."

Now, both our democracy and the world's climate are in mortal danger—under attack in an information war. We are in an epic struggle between two world views, two narratives, two stories—unity versus disunity. But the forces of disunity seem to have been winning of late, by "commanding the trend," using all the tools and strategies of virality to win elections, spread disinformation, and destroy our shared founding stories of unity.

There's no sitting out this struggle because the stakes are too high. You have to pick sides—unity or disunity. Will you tell stories that inspire and uplift listeners or ones that belittle and humiliate, to use the dichotomy of Dr. Lewis Mehl-Madrona from his 2005 book on Native American healing traditions, *Coyote Wisdom*? President Trump is certainly a master of the latter kind of stories. Indeed, a major reason I wrote this book was to explain the strategies of the forces of disunity and to help those fighting on the side of unity maximize your impact and become influence ninjas.

AMERICA'S STORY: PAST, PRESENT, AND FUTURE

Unity created out of diversity created this nation and then made it great. *E pluribus unum*—out of many, one—has been an official motto of the United States since 1782. "We must, indeed, all hang together, or most assuredly we shall all hang separately," as Ben Franklin said just before signing the Declaration of Independence.

As far back as the book of Genesis, God delivered the message that we do have a responsibility to look after each other. Cain is asked by the Lord, "Where is Abel thy brother?" Cain lies, "I know not: Am I my brother's keeper?" God replies angrily: "What hast thou done? the voice of thy brother's blood crieth unto me from the ground." By putting the line, "Am I my brother's keeper?" into the mouth of the first murderer, the Bible sends the message that we are our brother's keepers.

Unity and a shared understanding of the facts are our only hope in the arena I focus on—avoiding catastrophic global warming. We can prevent decades and then centuries of extreme drought, devastating sea level rise, superstorms, and deadly temperature rise leading to mass extinction, but only if the world works together to rapidly embrace clean energy and slash carbon pollution. That's why all of the major nations of the world, more than 190 in total, came together in Paris in December 2015 with pledges of serious action to restrict carbon pollution in the near term. That's why those nations unanimously agreed that, to avoid catastrophe, the world must keep ratcheting down emissions of carbon pollution until they are near or even below zero before century's end.

Disunity driven by disinformation is the guiding principle of those who oppose climate action. That's why those opponents have engaged in the gravest anti-science disinformation campaign in our history, dating back to the 1960s, funded by fossil fuel companies, and pushed by politicians like President Trump. That's why Trump, the embodiment of chaos and disunity who is backed by the major polluters, announced in June 2017 that he would withdraw the U.S. from the Paris Climate Accord.

The assault on science and on future generations is an attack on the heart of the Declaration of Independence and America's founding principles. This assault is a story that must be told and retold.

Jefferson's masterpiece famously begins, "When, in the course of human events, it becomes necessary for one people," to break free of tyranny and "assume among the powers of the earth, the separate and equal station to which the laws of Nature and of Nature's God entitle them," they should explain why they are impelled to do so:

> We hold these truths to be self-evident, that all men are created equal, that they are endowed by their Creator with certain unalienable rights, that among these are life, liberty and the pursuit of happiness.

The Declaration is a "scientific paper," explained historian Gary Wills in his 1978 book *Inventing America*. "The Declaration's opening is Newtonian. It lays down the law." Newton's landmark 1687 text, *Philosophiæ Naturalis Principia Mathematica* famously lays out his three laws of motion, which many at the time called the "laws of nature."

Jefferson was very familiar with the *Principia*. Newton's masterpiece was widely revered among the founding fathers. Jefferson once wrote a letter identifying a tiny mathematical error in it. He was very much a scientist at heart and once said, "Science is my passion, politics is my duty." For nearly two decades—including the entire time he was vice president and president—he was also president of the nation's oldest scientific society, The American Philosophical Society, founded by the great American scientist, Ben Franklin.

Jefferson and Franklin grounded the Declaration in the scientific laws of nature. That's clear from a crucial edit made by Franklin. As Historian Walter Isaacson explained in *Benjamin Franklin: An American Life*:

> The most important of his edits was small but resounding. He crossed out, using the heavy backslashes that he often employed, the last three words of Jefferson's phrase "We hold these truths to be sacred and undeniable" and changed them to the words now enshrined in history: "We hold these truths to be self-evident."

The idea of a "self-evident" truth drew from "the scientific determinism espoused by Isaac Newton and the analytic empiricism of Franklin's close friend David Hume," Isaacson noted. Hume referred to "truths that are so by virtue of reason and definition" as "self-evident" truths.

Today, it is the laws of nature, studied and enumerated by scientists, that make self-evident we are poised to render those unalienable rights unattainable for billions of humans on our current path of unrestricted carbon pollution. It is the laws of nature that make self-evident Americans can't achieve sustainable prosperity if the rest of the world doesn't. We are in this battle together.

Moreover, founding fathers such as Jefferson firmly believed we had an equal duty to future generations. Jefferson's September 1789 letter to James Madison, is "the most succinct, systematic treatment of intergenerational principles left to us by the founders," as The Constitutional

Law Foundation explains in its discussion of "Intergenerational Justice in the United States Constitution, The Stewardship Doctrine."

In this letter, Jefferson answers a crucial question: Must later generations "consider the preceding generation as having had a right to eat up the whole soil of their country, in the course of a life?" Soil was an obvious focal point for examining the issue of intergenerational equity for a Virginia planter like Jefferson.

The answer, to Jefferson, was another self-evident truth: *"Every one will say no; that the soil is the gift of God to the living, as much as it had been to the deceased generation."*

One generation destroying the next generation's vital soil or its livable climate is immoral. Hence it is horrifically immoral to flood their coastal soil and turn much of the rest into a permanent dust bowl. Yet that is what Trump's policies would put us on track to do according to the Congressionally mandated National Climate Assessment released in November 2017 after White House review and clearance.

"The catastrophic predictions now can no longer be looked on with contempt and irony," as Pope Francis said in his 195-page climate Encyclical Letter. "We can leave to future generations too many ruins, deserts and squalor." But "too many ruins, deserts, and squalor" is not an acceptable choice for a sane and moral society, as the Pope explained. We are not just our brothers' keepers but our children's.

THE HERO WITH A MILLION FACES

Before Joseph Campbell died in 1987, the journalist Bill Moyers interviewed him about *The Hero with a Thousand Faces*, which had become famous as a major inspiration for the original *Star Wars* trilogy. The resulting 1988 series,

The Power of Myth, was one of the most popular ever to air on PBS.

"Why the hero with a thousand faces?" Moyers asks in the first episode. "Well, because there is a certain typical hero sequence of actions, which can be detected in stories from all over the world, and from many, many periods of history," explains Campbell. "And I think it's essentially, you might say, the one deed done by many, many different people." Moyers naturally asks, "What is the deed?" Campbell answers:

> Well, there are two types of deed. One is the physical deed; the hero who has performed a war act or a physical act of heroism—saving a life, that's a hero act. Giving himself, sacrificing himself to another. And the other kind is the spiritual hero, who has learned or found a mode of experiencing the supernormal range of human spiritual life, and then come back and communicated it. It's a cycle, it's a going and a return, that the hero cycle represents.

In earlier chapters, I talked about my brother's journey, the going and return that he made, back to where my father was born, and, ultimately, to a place where he could let go of his anger. To my brother Danny and I, Dave's most heroic deed was establishing the Al Romm Interdisciplinary Journalism Scholarship Fund despite their often-bitter relationship. But the scholarship fund wasn't just a way to remember my father. It was a response to the election.

Here's what Dave wrote about the Fund, to which I will donate a quarter of the sales of this book:

> Qualifications include a) have to speak at least one language besides English fluently, 2) Must have gotten a B or better in an advanced math class and 3) worked on the HS newspaper or equivalent.

Established in the name of my father, A.N "Al" Romm, who was editor of the Middletown (NY) *Times Herald-Record*, it's for HS students in Orange County, NY.

My father often said he would rather hire a Political Science or History Major and teach them Journalism than hire a Journalism Major and teach them critical thinking.

This is partly in response to the last election. I'm laying groundwork for the future. I don't know what the US will look like in ten or fifteen years, but I'm hoping to help some kids gain some crucial skills.

If someone could write their own epitaph (from the Greek for "at" or "over" a "tomb"), then perhaps that should be his. In praising the heroes of Athens, Pericles said they had "the most splendid of sepulchers," a metaphorical tomb "where their glory remains eternal in men's minds, always there on the right occasion to stir others to speech or to action."

I wrote this book so that those who are stirred to speech and to action can also gain some crucial skills, reach millions, have the most impact, complete your hero's journey—and help others complete theirs.

SHOUTOUTS

This entire book is a shoutout to my brother Dave, and if it keeps his memory alive and helps inspire people "to speech or to action," then that is the smallest of repayments for the love, wisdom, and humor he shared with me and my daughter over the years.

My parents shared with me their non-pareil language and editing skills for decades—a debt I am obliged to pay forward. The inspirational nature of my mother, Ethel Grodzins Romm, beggars description and can't be fully understood until you meet her and she changes your life for the better, as she has for so many people, including me.

My brother Danny helped me immeasurably after Dave's death. And he's been a tremendous editor for this book. But he's also the reason I launched ClimateProgress. After his home was destroyed by Hurricane Katrina's storm surge in August 2005, he asked me for advice on whether he should rebuild. That led me to do a deep dive into climate science that made me realize our situation was much more dire than I (and 98% of opinion makers) realized. So I shifted away from helping companies embrace clean energy and climate solutions—and became a full-time communicator.

I am forever grateful to everyone at the Center for American Progress Action Fund (CAPAF) for enabling that shift, for believing in the idea of ClimateProgress.org, and for supporting the website over the years as it grew and merged into ThinkProgress.org. I especially thank John Podesta and Neera Tanden and Judd Legum. I owe a debt to so many people who provided advice and support over the years, including Sean Pool, Kari Manlove, Brad Johnson, Faiz Shakir, Nico Pitney, Stephen Lacey, Andrew Sherry, Dan Weiss, Ryan Koronowski, Sam Page, Kyla Mandel, and Kiley Kroh. A special shoutout goes to the social media mavens of ThinkProgress—Phoebe Gavin, Frank Dale, and Patrick Smith—for teaching me so much of what I know about going viral.

I am so thankful for the amazing producers of *Years of Living Dangerously*, particularly Joel Bach, James Cameron, David Gelber, and Maria Wilhelm. I've learned most of what I know about viral videos and visual storytelling from them.

I greatly appreciate the New Frontier Data team for patiently explaining how big data works and what kind of stories it can tell—especially Giadha De Carcer, Gary Allen, Rami Mansour, Gretchen Gailey, and John Kagia. And I owe a great debt to Carl Cameron, for helping me connect the dots on how the Russians coordinated their cyberattack and their messaging with the Trump campaign in 2016.

A very loud shoutout goes to both Adam Gilad and Randy Olson for bringing their unique combination of storytelling and marketing skills to this manuscript. Their comments greatly improved the final product. So did the comments of viral writer and master editor David Wallace-Wells. I'm also very grateful that Ann Friedman brought her tremendous language skills to bear on the final draft, and that Stacy Whittle shared with me her unmatched marketing skills. Also, I feel very lucky that Daria Musk shared with me her amazing story.

I'd like to thank the team at Luminare Press led by Patricia Marshall—including Kim Harper-Kennedy, Bronwynn Dean, and Claire Flint Last—for making the process of turning my manuscript into a book so painless, especially on such a tight deadline. And I'd also like to thank Jeff Bezos for disrupting the publishing industry and creating a distribution platform that lets writers keep most of the profit of their work.

Finally, I hope the stories in this book give readers a glimpse of some of the magical insight and inspiration I am blessed to get on a regular basis from my daughter, Antonia. I can't imagine this book would have been written had I not seen the world anew through her eyes and her imagination. Ultimately, it is the Antonias around the world who we must all bear in mind when we contemplate the consequences of our action—and our inaction—in the fights against climate change and Trumpism.

REFERENCES

NOTE: References that are identified in the text (by, for example the title of the article or title of the book) are generally not repeated here.

References to the Bible generally follow the King James Version. References to Shakespeare plays generally follow the act, scene, and line numbers of *The Riverside Shakespeare*, textual editor, G. Blakemore Evans (Boston: Houghton Mifflin, 1974).

INTRODUCTION

Frenkel, Sheera and Katie Benner. 2018. "To Stir Discord in 2016, Russians Turned Most Often to Facebook." *The New York Times*, February 17, 2018.

Gottschall, Jonathan. 2013. *The Storytelling Animal*. New York, NY: Mariner Books.

Vedantam, Shankar. 2007. "Persistence of Myths Could Alter Public Policy Approach." *The Washington Post*, September 4, 2007.

CHAPTER ONE

Axelrod, Mark. 2016. "Trump 2016: Deconstructing Donny; or The Rhetoric of Nonsense, Part II." *Huffington Post*, August 3, 2016.

Berger, Jonah and Katherine Milkman. 2012. "What Makes Online Content Viral?" *Journal of Marketing Research*, April 2012.

Groden, Claire. 2015. "Donald Trump Would Be Richer If He'd Have Invested in Index Funds." *Fortune*, August 20, 2015.

Karnie, Annie. 2016. "Has Hillary Finally Found Her Voice?" *Politico*, July 15, 2016.

Leith, Sam. 2015. "Trump Shows Speech Can Have Effect Without Making Complete Sense." *Financial Times*, June 22, 2015.

Peacham, Henry. 1593. *The Garden of Eloquence.* Gainseville, FL: Scholars' Facimilies & Reprints, 1954.

Penzenstadler, Nick and Susan Page. 2016. "Exclusive: Trump's 3,500 Lawsuits Unprecedented for a Presidential Nominee." *USA Today*, June 1, 2016.

CHAPTER TWO

Basler, Roy P. 1973. *A Touchstone for Greatness.* Westport, CT: Greenwood Press.

Olson, Randy. 2015. *Houston, We Have A Narrative: Why Science Needs Story.* Chicago: University of Chicago Press.

Poniewozikjan, James. 2018. "What Politicians Could Learn From Oprah Winfrey." *The New York Times*, January 8, 2018.

CHAPTER THREE

Abbruzzese, Jason. 2016. "Donald Trump Has the Grammar of a Fifth Grader, Study Says." Mashable.com, March 20, 2016.

Liberman, Mark. 2011. "Up in Ur Internets, Shortening All the Words." *Language Log* blog, University of Pennsylvania, October 28, 2011.

CHAPTER FOUR

Allen, Mike and Jim Vandehei. 2005. "Social Security Push to Tap the GOP Faithful." *The Washington Post*, January 14, 2005.

Hashe, Lynn et al., 1977. "Frequency and the Conference of Referential Validity." *Journal of Verbal Learning and Verbal Behavior*, February 1977.

Keller, Bill. 2003. "The Radical Presidency of George W. Bush." *New York Times Magazine*, January 26, 2003.

Murphy, Dean. 2005. "If You Can Plug a Film, Why Not a Budget?" *The New York Times,* February 13, 2005.

CHAPTER FIVE

Cuddon, J. A. 1977. *A Dictionary of Literary Terms*. Garden City, NY: Doubleday.

Emery, Daniel. 2009. "Joke Review Boosts T-shirt Sales." *BBC News*, May 21, 2009.

Perlman, Merrill. "Irony Patch." *Columbia Journalism Review*, July 18, 2011.

Purdy, Jedidiah. 1999. *For Common Things*. New York: Vintage Books.

Sedgewick, G. G. 1935. *Of Irony.* Toronto: University of Toronto Press.

Andrews, John, editor. 1995. *Othello (Everyman's Library)*. London: J. M. Dent.

CHAPTER SIX

O'Harrow Jr., Robert and Shawn Boburg. 2016. "The Man Who Showed Donald Trump How to Exploit Power and Instill Fear." *The Washington Post*, June 17, 2016.

Sloman, Steven A. 2002. "Two Systems of Reasoning." In *Heuristics and Biases*, edited by Thomas Gilovich et al. Cambridge, UK: Cambridge University Press.

CHAPTER SEVEN

Hessan, Diane. 2016. "Understanding the Undecided Voters." *The Boston Globe*, November 21, 2016.

Kahneman, Daniel and Shane Frederick. 2002. "Representativeness Revisited." In *Heuristics and Biases,* edited by Thomas Gilovich et al. Cambridge, UK: Cambridge University Press.

Reynolds, Ralph E. and Robert M. Schwartz. 1983. "Relation of Metaphoric Processing to Comprehension and Memory." *Journal of Educational Psychology*, Vol. 75, June 1983.

CHAPTER EIGHT

Green, Joshua and Sasha Issenberg. 2016. "Inside the Trump Bunker, With Days to Go." Bloomberg.com, October 27, 2016.

Haile, Tony. 2014. "What You Think You Know About the Web Is Wrong." Time.com, March 9, 2014.

Rosenberg, Matthew. 2018. "How Trump Consultants Exploited the Facebook Data of Millions." *The New York Times*, March 17, 2018.

Scola, Nancy. 2017. "How Facebook, Google and Twitter 'Embeds' Helped Trump in 2016." Politico.com, October 26, 2017.

CHAPTER NINE

Vena, Jocelyn. 2011. "Lady Gaga Says 'Judas' Video 'Celebrates Faith.'" MTV.com, April 26, 2011.

CHAPTER TEN

Adamson, Allen. 2014. "Disney Knows It's Not Just Magic That Keeps a Brand on Top." *Forbes*, October 15, 2014.

Higbey, Tomas. 2013. "What Are the Best Stories About People Randomly (or Non-randomly) Meeting Steve Jobs?" Quora.com, July 1, 2013.

CHAPTER 11

Demirjian, Karoun and Devlin Barrett. 2017. "How a Dubious Russian Document Influenced the FBI's Handling of the Clinton Probe." *The Washington Post*, May 24, 2017.

Eichenwald, Kurt. 2017. "Trump, Putin and the Hidden History of How Russia Interfered in the U.S. Presidential Election." *Newsweek*, January 10, 2017.

Kaczynski, Andrew and Gloria Borger. 2018. "Stone, On Day he Sent Assange Dinner Email, Also Said 'Devastating' WikiLeaks Were Forthcoming." CNN.com, April 4, 2018.

Kaczynski, Andrew, Nathan McDermott, and Chris Massie. 2017. "Trump Adviser Roger Stone Repeatedly Claimed to Know of Forthcoming WikiLeaks Dumps." CNN.com, March 20, 2017.

Parker, Ashley and John Wagner. 2018. "'Go Donald!': Inside the Russian Shadow Campaign to Elect Trump." *The Washington Post*, February 16, 2018.

Poulsen, Kevin and Spencer Ackerman. 2018. "EXCLUSIVE: 'Lone DNC Hacker' Guccifer 2.0 Slipped Up and Revealed He Was a Russian Intelligence Officer." TheDailyBeast.com, March 22, 2018.

Silverman, Craig. 2016. "This Analysis Shows How Viral Fake Election News Stories Outperformed Real News On Facebook." BuzzFeed.com, November 16, 2016.

Troianovski, Anton. 2018. "A Former Russian Troll Speaks: 'It was like being in Orwell's world.'" *The Washington Post*, February 17, 2018.

Index

A

ABT 29, 32 – 37, 40 – 43, 64
Amazon 76, 163 – 166, 168
And-But-Therefore 4, 30, 155, 199. *See also* ABT
Antony, Marc 78, 79, 81
Aristotle 6, 17, 19, 20, 21, 25, 59, 111, 163
Assange, Julian 195, 196, 219

B

"Bad Romance" (Lady Gaga) 158
Bezos, Jeff 107, 163, 164, 213
Bible, King James 25, 39, 51, 68
big data 10 – 14, 132, 138, 142 – 145, 184, 200, 213
Bond, James 70
branding 20, 26, 29, 61, 106, 167, 171 – 174
Bush, George W. 54, 81, 217

C

Cambridge Analytica 145 – 147, 172, 184
Cameron, Carl 147, 182, 184, 195, 213
Cameron, James 12, 86, 148, 151, 165
Campbell, Joseph 30, 108, 204, 209
Character, personal 163
Churchill, Winston 43, 50, 118, 200
Cicero 21, 22, 25, 26
Cillizza, Chris 122
Citizen Kane 147, 183, 184, 195, 213
Cleese, John 70, 92, 127
climate change (see also global warming) 2, 12, 13, 62 – 65,
    150 – 155, 164, 181, 214
ClimateProgress 10, 11, 15, 137, 139, 140, 151, 188, 212
Clinton, Bill 55, 87, 91
Clinton, Hillary 3, 23, 38, 54, 63, 80, 120 – 122, 145, 186, 192, 197
Comey, James 123, 185

D

Daily Show, The 83, 84
Dawkins, Richard 1, 59, 160
Disney 169, 218
Dylan, Bob 52, 86

E

eulogy 9, 16, 42, 71, 72, 79, 92, 93, 109, 112, 127, 205
extended metaphor 30, 43, 113 – 121, 125, 127, 128, 158

F

Facebook 1, 2, 11, 13, 14, 49, 131 – 137, 143 – 146, 149, 153, 168, 171, 172, 187, 194, 215, 218, 219
Fifty Shades of Gray 165
figures of speech (see individual figures)
foreshadowing 47, 95 – 109

G

Gale, Dorothy 109
Gelber, David 13, 150, 152, 213
Gettysburg Address 42, 69, 71, 100, 113, 125
Gilad, Adam 166, 179, 213
global warming 18, 206, 221
Google 11, 71, 92, 137, 145, 168, 175 – 177, 218
Gorgias 17 – 25, 27, 64
Guccifer2.0 183, 195, 196

H

Hamill, Mark 133, 203
Hamilton 2, 6, 30, 95 – 98, 112, 159, 202
Hamlet 40 – 45, 51, 70, 89, 116
healthcare reform 173
Hemingway, Ernest 56, 57
Hero with a Thousand Faces, The 30, 47, 108, 209
Homer 5, 30, 177
hyperbole 5, 6, 17 – 20, 107, 122, 124

I

Iago 26, 65, 66, 82
"I have a dream" speech 69, 99 – 103
Internet Research Agency 189, 193
Irony
  dramatic irony 81 – 88
  poetic justice 89 – 91
  Socratic irony 77 – 78
  verbal irony 78 – 80

J

Jefferson, Thomas 207, 208, 209
Jesus 2, 21, 29, 32, 34, 37, 39, 44, 69, 70, 71, 101, 102, 113
Jobs, Steve 107, 163, 169, 178, 218
John, Elton 112
Julius Caesar 49, 50, 78, 96, 99, 127

K

Kennedy, John F. 118
King, Martin Luther 2, 32, 62, 69, 99, 103

L

Lakoff, George 111, 115
Language Intelligence 5, 22, 164, 165, 201
Lincoln, Abraham 2, 21, 29, 32, 34, 41 – 45, 62, 69, 71, 78, 99, 100,
        113, 118, 127, 184, 205
logographos 25
Logos 39, 71
Luntz, Frank 50, 59, 173, 188

M

McCain, John 81, 120
meme 1, 59, 60, 65, 77, 80, 112, 160, 189
metaphor 4, 5, 8, 30, 40, 43, 59, 77, 101, 111 – 128, 140 – 141, 149,
        153, 156, 158, 159, 190, 199
Miranda, Lin-Manuel 2, 6, 30, 95, 112
Mueller, Robert 146, 184, 191, 194, 197, 198
Musk, Daria 168, 174, 213

N

New Frontier Data 10, 13, 142, 147, 213

O

Obama, Barack 2, 55, 80, 81, 106, 114, 120 – 122, 141, 173, 174
Ogilvy, David 131, 133
Orwell, George 49, 91, 190, 219
Othello 65, 82, 217

P

Palin, Sarah 120, 121
Parscale, Brad 11, 131, 144, 145, 193
pattern matching 8, 36, 98, 112
Pixar 169, 179
Pope Francis 187, 203, 209
Potter, Harry 29, 31, 45, 96, 109, 166

Q

Quixote, Don 84, 93

R

repetition
  chiasmus 70, 118, 141
Romney, Mitt 80, 121, 122, 123
Russians 1, 3, 11, 14, 80, 138, 183 – 199, 213, 215

S

Schwarzenegger 67, 152
Seinfeld 75, 82, 89
Shakespeare 2, 21 – 26, 32, 34, 41 – 46, 50, 51, 65, 66, 70, 76, 78, 82,
        88, 90, 96 – 99, 102, 103, 116, 127, 215
60 Minutes 13, 91, 131, 144, 149 – 153
Skywalker, Luke 29, 31, 45, 91, 109, 204
slogans 49, 53, 55, 60, 61, 117, 146, 173
Star Wars 25, 30, 46, 91, 108, 209
Stewart, Jon 22, 83
stories, viral 76, 187
Swift, Taylor 30, 157, 159

T

Taylor, Jerry 181
testing
  headlines 11, 139, 142
  messages 4, 11, 131, 132, 138, 144, 147, 200
ThinkProgress 10, 11, 132, 133, 135, 137, 138, 196, 204, 212, 213
Titanic 86, 151, 152
Trump 2 – 6, 9, 11, 14, 17 – 23, 26, 27, 32, 38, 49, 50, 55, 56, 61 – 65,
        75, 80, 84, 85, 106, 107, 113, 115, 119, 122 – 127, 131, 132,
        138, 143 – 150, 156, 172, 173, 179 – 199, 205 – 209, 213 – 219
Twitter 2, 11, 137, 140, 141, 145, 168, 172, 191, 195, 218

V

videos, viral 13, 76, 96, 154, 156, 159, 213

W

warming, global 18, 206
WikiLeaks 183, 187, 189, 191, 195 – 197, 219
Winfrey, Oprah 32, 34, 72, 128, 216
Wizard of Oz, The 29, 31

Y

Years Project, The 10, 13, 149, 150, 154
YouTube 5, 75, 153, 156, 159, 166, 168, 178

Z

Zuckerberg, Mark 171, 172

Made in the USA
Middletown, DE
06 June 2018